4 YEAR

Classworks
Literacy

Sue Plechowicz

Acknowledgements

The author and publishers wish to thank the following for permission to use copyright material:

'Big Billy' by Peter Dixon, reprinted by permission of Macmillan Children's Books, London.

'My Brother Bert' from *Meet My Folks* by Ted Hughes, reprinted by permission of Faber and Faber Ltd.

Carrie's War by Nina Bawden (Puffin, 1974). Copyright Nina Bawden, 1973. Reproduced by permission of Penguin Books Limited.

'Night Fishing' © Moira Andrew, first published in *A Glass of Fresh Air*, edited by Moira Andrew, Collins Educational, 1996.

Street Child © Berlie Doherty. Reprinted by permission of HarperCollins Publishers Ltd.

Calling All Sleepyheads from *Have Your Say* by Karavis & Matthews. Reprinted by permission of Harcourt Education Ltd.

'Persecution', from *Judaism* by Sue Penney. Reprinted by permission of Harcourt Education Ltd.

'Lothlorien' from *The Lord of the Rings: The Fellowship of the Ring Visual Companion* © Jude Fisher/J R R Tolkien. Reprinted by permission of HarperCollins Publishers Ltd

'The Day's Eye' © Pie Corbett, printed by permission of the author.

'Charlie and the Chocolate Factory' by Roald Dahl, from *Charlie and the Chocolate Factory – a Play*, an adaptation by Richard George, reprinted by permission of David Higham Associates.

Bad Girls by Jacqueline Wilson, published by Doubleday. Reprinted by permission of the Random House Group Ltd.

'The Sun' by Grace Nichols, acknowledgement to Curtis Brown Group Ltd. on behalf of Grace Nichols © Grace Nichols 1988.

'Classrooms' from *Harry Potter & The Prisoner of Azkaban* © JK Rowling 1999.

'The Troll' by Jack Prelutsky, from *Nightmares – Poems to Trouble Your Sleep*, reprinted by permission of A&C Black Publishers Ltd.

The Busy Day © Margaret Cooling, from *Story & Drama Toolkit*, published by British & Foreign Bible Society 1996.

The Abradizil by Andrew Gibson, reprinted by permission of Faber & Faber Ltd.

Extract from *The Camera Obscura* © 1990 Hugh Scott. Reproduced by permission of Walker Books Ltd., London SE11 5HJ.

Raiders by Lynne Benton © Lynne Benton 1998. Reprinted by permission of Harcourt Education Limited.

A Jumble for a Queen by Julia Donaldson © Julia Donaldson 1998. Reprinted by permission of Harcourt Eduation Linited.

Cover photo by Andy Sotirious/Getty Images.

Every effort has been made to trace the copyright holders but if any have been inadvertently overlooked the publishers will be pleased to make the necessary arrangement at the first opportunity.

Contents

Unit	Outcome	Objectives	Page
Character Sketches	Character sketches for a story set during World War Two, with a curricular link to history	S1, S3, S4, S4 T1, T2, T11	1
Persuasive Writing	A persuasive letter to the head teacher on a school-related issue; an advertisement or poster persuading other children to read more books	S3, S4 T18, T19, T20, T23, T25	16
Classic and Modern Poetry	Poems written in the style of those read; performance of own and others' poems	S1 T4, T6, T7, T11	33
Narrative Writing Using Paragraphs	A story written in paragraphs from a plan, set in World War Two (curricular links to history)	S1, S2, S4, S5 T1, T3, T4, T9, T10, T12, T15	48
Poetry on a Common Theme	Poetry based on personal or imagined experience	S3, S4 T7, T8, T14	65
Instructions	Ability to give and follow clear instructions; a mathematical game	S1 T22, T25, T26	81
Playscripts	Playscript developed and extended by the class for performance	S3, S4 T5, T6, T13	90
Stories That Raise Issues	A short story about a dilemma; writing about how an issue may affect a character	S1 T1, T3, T8, T9, T11	105
Newspapers and Reports	A report for a class newpaper (compiled in ICT lessons); a non-chronological report; discussion and prediction of stories from headlines	S1, S2, S5 T16, T17, T18, T19, T20, T21, T24, T27	119
Stories about Imagined Worlds	Fantasy settings making use of expressive and descriptive language	S1 T1, T2, T3, T4, T5, T10, T13	140
Stories in Stories	A book (with the story in chapters) for a younger audience	S2, S4 T3, T9, T12, T13, T14	154
Explanations and Information Books	A class wall chart on the course of a river; an explanation of the water cycle; a talk, using notes, about one of these	S3, S4 T15, T16, T17, T18, T19, T20, T21, T22, T23, T24, T25	171
Discussion Texts	Points of view, sequenced in a writing frame, ready for a presentation or debate; a discussion text	S4 T16, T17, T21, T22, T24	187

Introduction

How Classworks works

What this book contains

- Chunks of text, both annotated and 'blank' for your own annotations.
- Checklists (or toolkits), planning frames, storyboards, scaffolds and other writing aids.
- Examples of modelled, supported and demonstration writing.
- Lesson ideas including key questions and plenary support.
- Marking ladders for structured self-assessment.
- Blocked unit planning with suggested texts, objectives and outcomes.
- Word-level starter ideas to complement the daily teaching of phonics, handwriting and other skills.
- There are no scripts, no worksheets and nothing you can't change to suit your needs.

How this book is organised

- There are blocked units of work (see previous page) lasting between one week and several, depending on the text type.
- Each blocked unit is organised into a series of chunks of teaching content.
- Each 'chunk' has accompanying checklists and other photocopiable resources.
- For every text we *suggest* annotations, checklists and marking ladders.
- Every unit follows the *teaching sequence for writing* found in *Grammar for Writing* (DfES, 2001, 2000).
- You can mix and match teaching ideas, units and checklists as you see fit.

How you can use *Classworks* with your medium-term plan

- Refer to your medium-term planning for the blocking of NLS objectives.
- Find the text-type you want to teach (or just the objectives).
- Use the contents page to locate the relevant unit.
- Familiarise yourself with the text and language features using *Classworks* checklists and exemplar analysis pages, and DfES or QCA resources such as *Grammar for Writing*.
- Browse the lesson ideas and photocopiables to find what you want to use.
- You can just use the text pages … photocopy and adapt the checklists … use or change some of the teaching ideas … take whatever you want and adapt it to fit your class.

Planning a blocked unit of work with Classworks

Classworks units exemplify a blocked unit approach to planning the teaching of Literacy. What follows is an outline of this method of planning and teaching, and how *Classworks* can help you

You need: *Classworks* Literacy Year 4, medium-term planning; OHT (optional).
Optional resources: your own choice of texts for extra analysis; *Grammar for Writing*.

Method

- From the medium-term planning, identify the **outcome**, **texts** and **objectives** you want to teach.

- *Classworks* units **exemplify** how some units could be planned, resourced and taught.

- Decide how to 'chunk' the text you are analysing, for example, introductory paragraph, paragraph 1, paragraph 2, closing paragraph.

- *Classworks* units give an example of **chunking** with accompanying resources and exemplar analysis. Texts for pupil analysis (labelled 'Pupil copymaster') are intended for whole class display on an OHT.

- **Whatever you think of the checklists provided, analyse the text with *your* class and build *your own* checklist for the whole text, and for each chunk.**

- Plan your blocked unit based on the following teaching sequence for writing.

- *Classworks* units outline one way of planning a **blocked unit**, with exemplifications of some days, and suggestions for teaching content on others.

Shared Reading – analysing the text – create 'checklist' or writer's toolkit	The children analyse another of that text type and add to checklist	Review checklist
Shared Writing – demonstrate application of 'checklist' to a small piece of writing	The children write independently based on your demonstration	Use examples on OHT to check against the 'checklist'

- This model is only a guideline, allowing the writing process to be scaffolded. You would want to build in opportunities for planning for writing, talking for writing, teaching explicit word-level and sentence-level objectives that would then be modelled in the shared writing, and so on. There are ideas for word-level and sentence-level starters on pages 200–201.

- Allow opportunities for the children to be familiar with the text type. This might include reading plenty of examples, drama, role play, video, and so on.

Assessment

- Make sure that 'checklists' are displayed around the room and referred to before writing and when assessing writing in the **plenary**.

- One or two children could work on an OHT and this could be the focus of the plenary.

- Use a **marking ladder** for the children to evaluate their writing. This is based on the checklist your class has built up. We give you an example of how it might look for each blocked unit. There's a blank copy on page 202.

What each page does

Text-type written large at the top, and then on every page.

What a unit based on this material might look like.

Shaded sections refer to *Classworks* ideas, white sections to suggested extra content.

Text-based outcome clearly signalled.

Objectives spelt out.

Key aspects of teaching this text type listed.

Child-friendly outcomes for every chunk of content.

Clear headings for each section of the page.

Main idea broken up into bullets and key questions.

Board-work examples highlighted clearly.

Classworks resources referenced wherever relevant.

Brief independent, pair or guided work idea.

Plenary guidance.

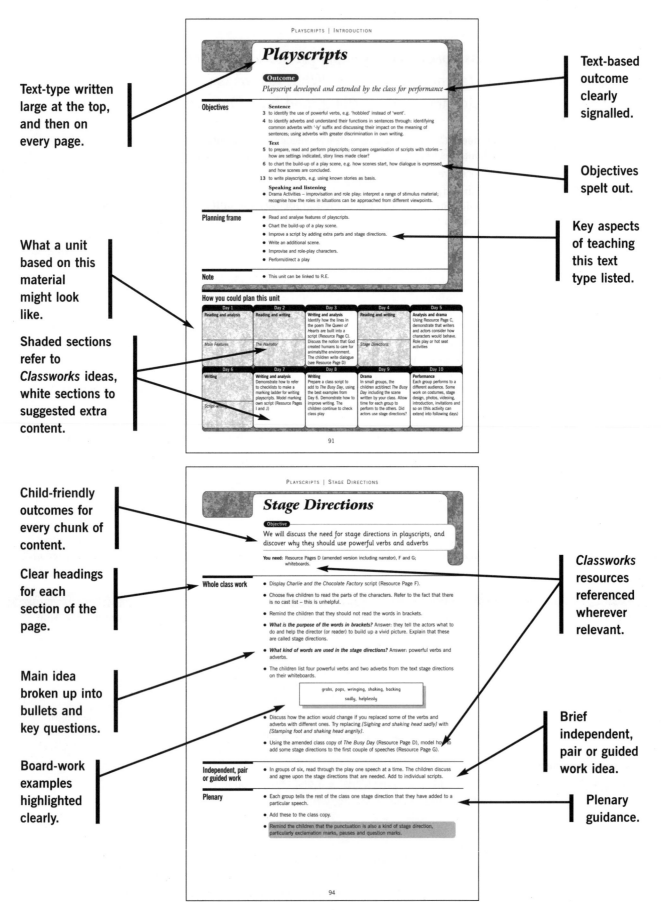

Character Sketches

Outcome

Character sketches for a story set during World War Two, with a curricular link to history

Objectives

Sentence

1 to revise and extend work on adjectives from Year 3 term 2 and link to work on expressive language in stories and poetry.

3 to identify the use of powerful verbs, e.g. 'hobbled' instead of 'went', e.g. through cloze procedure.

4 to identify adverbs and understand their functions in sentences through: identifying common adverbs with '-ly' suffix and discussing their impact on the meaning of sentences; collecting and classifying examples of adverbs; investigating the effects of substituting adverbs in clauses or sentences; using adverbs with greater discrimination in own writing.

4 to use speech marks and other dialogue punctuation appropriately and to use the conventions which mark boundaries between spoken words and the rest of the sentence. [Year 3 objective]

Text

1 to investigate how settings and characters are built up from small details, and how the reader responds to them.

2 to identify the main characteristics of key characters, drawing on the text to justify views, and using the information to predict actions.

11 to write character sketches, focusing on small details to evoke sympathy or dislike.

Planning frame

- Make a class word bank of verbs to use instead of 'went' and 'said'.
- Read and identify how authors use adjectives and adjectival phrases to help build up special details of a character's appearance.
- Understand what makes dialogue between characters effective.
- Know that a good start for planning a character is choosing a specific 'type'.

How you could plan this unit

Day 1	Day 2	Day 3	Day 4	Day 5
Reading and writing Understand the concept of powerful verbs. Make powerful verb bank for display – words to use instead of 'went' and 'said'	Reading and analysis	Reading and analysis	Reading and writing	Reading and analysis
	Powerful Verbs and Adverbs	*Using Adjectives*	*Choosing Names*	*Use of Speech*

Day 6	Day 7	Day 8	Day 9	Day 10
Speaking and listening Characterisation through what is said. In pairs, the children write a dialogue. Plenary: act out conversations	**Writing** Identify character types/ stereotypes. Use spidergraph to model brainstorming how a 'type' could be portrayed, e.g. 'sporty'. The children compile own spidergraph for a character type	**Writing** *Writing a Sketch*	**Writing** Model turning character plans into a character sketch (see Example 2, Resource Page H). The children plan and write sketch for their own character	**Reading and analysis** Evaluate character sketch using marking ladder (Resource Page I). You could watch part of *Goodnight Mr Tom* on video. Focus on how Mr Tom is developed over the first few scenes

1

Powerful Verbs and Adverbs

Objective

We will identify powerful verbs and adverbs and discuss why they are good to use in descriptions

You need: Resource Pages A, B and H; whiteboards; highlighters.

Whole class work

- Read these sentence starters aloud: 'She came into the room and said ...'; 'Holly stomped noisily into the kitchen and yelled ...'

- Discuss which sentence tells us more about the character.

- Establish that the second sentence is more effective because it uses powerful verbs and an adverb, both of which give hints about the character and how she is feeling.

- *When writers describe the way their character is talking or moving, they use powerful verbs and adverbs to give the reader more details about the character and the way the character is feeling at that moment. This is much more effective than just telling the reader that Holly was angry.*

- Read the first half of *Raiders!* (Resource Page A), asking the children to note, on their whiteboards, some of the powerful verbs and adverbs the writer uses to describe the way the characters speak or move. **Can you guess what the characters are like and the way they are feeling?**

- From the answers given, begin to compile a class checklist (see Resource Page H for ideas).

Independent, pair or guided work

- The children highlight powerful verbs and adverbs in *Raiders!* (see Resource Page B) and note what they reveal about the character and the character's feelings.

Plenary

- Write on the board:

> Susan _____ into the room.
>
> She _____ into the chair, stared around and _____ thought about why she felt so _____ .

- Tell the children that you are going to fill in the last blank with a feeling. The children suggest verbs and adverbs to fit in the other spaces, for example:

> Susan <u>skipped cheerfully</u> into the room.
>
> She <u>bounced</u> into the chair, stared around and <u>gleefully</u> thought about why she felt so <u>happy</u>.

Using Adjectives

Objective

We will revise adjectives and use interesting language in stories

You need: Resource Pages C and D; a selection of pictures of people taken from magazines or books; whiteboards.

Whole class work

- Read the excerpt from *Street Child* on Resource Page C and discuss the characters. ***What picture do you have in your head of the matron and Jim and Joseph? What was it in the text that helped you to build the picture?*** You may need to explain the job that the matron will do, for example, order the food, care for the children, discipline them, and so on.

- Establish that, as well as powerful verbs, it is adjectives that give us special details about the character's appearance and enable us to visualise him or her. ***Adjectives help us to determine what kind of character they are, for example, a goody or a baddy.***

- Look at some pictures of people taken from magazines/books. Ask the children to write on their whiteboards some adjectives that describe their appearance.

- ***What kind of person would a stranger think you are?***

Independent, pair or guided work

- In pairs, the children highlight the adjectives and adjectival phrases in the text, and note down what they reveal about the character.

Plenary

- Use an enlarged copy of the excerpt from *Carrie's War* (Resource Page D). Read and discuss. ***Do you think there is any information in this description that is not needed for the story? Why do you think the author included it?***

- Establish the fact that there is too much detail. In fact the only important description is that 'he wasn't an ogre'.

- Explain that giving too much distracting description of appearance slows down the story. Authors have to achieve a balance between painting a picture with words and maintaining the pace of the story.

Choosing Names

Objective

We will investigate how characters' names can be used to identify their 'type'

You need: Resource Pages C–E; whiteboards.

Whole class work

- Review the checklist and remind the children about how authors build up characters through the use of details. Emphasise that these are added to as the story develops and are not often introduced all at once.

- Point out that authors usually introduce the character with a name. *A carefully chosen name can tell you a lot about how a character is likely to behave and allows the reader to predict what might happen.*

- Explain that you are going to read some extracts from stories and that you want the children to say why they are interesting and to predict what they think the characters will be like.

- Read the excerpts from *Street Child* (Resource Pages C and D). In pairs, the children discuss some of the characters' names. Allow only 30 seconds for each name and then discuss as a whole group.

- Using whiteboards, ask the children to make up names for new characters.

Independent, pair or guided work

- The children match the names to the descriptions, using Resource Page E.

- Using the following names, the children predict what kind of character may have been given each name:

> Buster Brown
>
> Mr Stonehouse
>
> Mrs Goody
>
> Joy Jollysmith
>
> Slugger Smith

Plenary

- Share some of the children's ideas. *Which names tell you most about the character type?*

4

Use of Speech

Objective

We will investigate how writers develop characters through speech

You need: Resource Page F; highlighters.

Whole class work	• Explain that the focus of this lesson is to examine how writers develop characters through speech: what they say and how they say it.

> monologue = one person speaking
>
> dialogue = two people speaking (from the Greek 'logos' meaning word)

• Read the excerpt from *Not Always a Perfect Place* (Resource Page F). **What do you think Beatrice and Olivia are like? Why do you think that? What evidence is there in the text to support your comment?**

• Point out that the things the characters said and did may lead us to judge Olivia as being kind, caring and brave but Beatrice as being uncaring, nervous and a snob. **What words or phrases could be changed to make Beatrice sound nicer?**

• Beatrice and Olivia's clothes aren't described in the extract. **What do you think their clothes might be like? How do you know this? Why didn't the author need to put it in the extract?** Answer: the reader still gets a mental 'picture' about the way the girls look, so describing their clothing would be adding unnecessary detail at this point.

Independent, pair or guided work

• The children highlight the speech and action in different colours and consider what this tells the reader about the characters.

• **What other information is there in the text that tells the reader about the personality of the characters?**

• Choosing a small section of the dialogue, the children rewrite it in 'modern' language.

Plenary

• Share some work. Point out that when writing a story you should plan the speech and action so that these are appropriate to your characters. **Would the boy in the extract say, 'My shower is broken'? Why not?**

Writing a Sketch

Objective

We will write our own character sketch, focusing on small details to evoke sympathy or dislike

You need: Resource Pages G and H; non-fiction books about World War Two.

Whole class work

- Go through the checklist for writing character sketches (see Resource Page H) and explain that you are going to model how to plan a character for a story set in World War Two, using the checklist to guide you.

- Model writing a planning frame (Resource Page G), commenting why you are including each detail, for example: *I think I will write that he has a pale, tear-stained face because that will show that he is sad ... that he creeps silently and watches every movement in the room because that will hint that he is scared.*

- When you have completed your plan ask the children to check that you have included all the things on the checklist.

- Point out that the purpose of planning the characters is so that you can use the plan to refer back to later. *TV fiction programmes like* **Buffy the Vampire Slayer** *have character 'bibles' that include information about the character for each episode so that the writers don't make a mistake about who her friends are, how she speaks, which school/college she goes to, what she likes/dislikes and so on.*

Independent, pair or guided work

- Using the planning frame and referring to the checklist as a guide, the children write a plan for a character to be used in a story set in World War Two.

Plenary

- Share some of the character plans and evaluate them using a response sandwich: one good comment, followed by an idea on how to improve the work, followed by a second good comment.

(**Pupil copymaster**)

Raiders!

Trying desperately to keep out of sight, I wriggle backwards until I cannot see the raiders any more. Then I leap to my feet and start to run, faster than I have ever run in my life. My feet skim over the rough grass.

My heart is pounding, and I am terrified, but I dare not stop. I have to warn them. Only when I reach the fence do I dare to look over my shoulder. The raiders are not in sight yet, but I know they cannot be far behind. I run inside and bar the gate. Then I race to the nearest hut and bang on the door.

"Raiders!" I shout. "Help! Raiders! Help!"

I don't wait for an answer, but run to the next hut.

"Raiders!"

I can hear people stirring behind me as I race through the village. I cannot stop until I have warned Father.

Suddenly I hear a loud splintering noise behind me as the raiders attack the gate with their axes. Then they surge into the village, with terrible, bloodcurdling cries.

As I reach our hut, the door opens and Father comes out brandishing his sword.

"Well done, Edric," he cries. "We're ready for them!"

Then I realise everyone is awake. There is a lot of shouting and the clash of swords and spears. We Anglo-Saxons may not be as big as them, but we are fierce when we're threatened. We won't give in without a fight.

"Look after your mother and sister, Edric," calls Father as he charges into battle. The noise is deafening now. I turn and see other women and children huddled at the fence, away from the fighting.

from Raiders!, *by Lynne Benton*

(Exemplar analysis)

Example of analysis of *Raiders!*

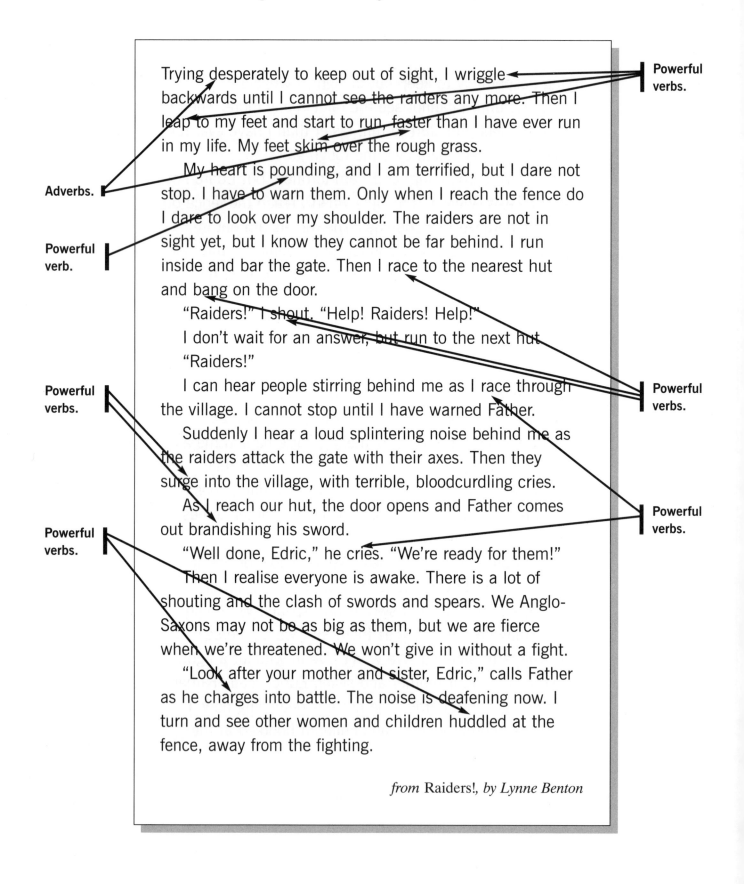

Trying desperately to keep out of sight, I wriggle
backwards until I cannot see the raiders any more. Then I
leap to my feet and start to run, faster than I have ever run
in my life. My feet skim over the rough grass.

My heart is pounding, and I am terrified, but I dare not
stop. I have to warn them. Only when I reach the fence do
I dare to look over my shoulder. The raiders are not in
sight yet, but I know they cannot be far behind. I run
inside and bar the gate. Then I race to the nearest hut
and bang on the door.

"Raiders!" I shout. "Help! Raiders! Help!"
I don't wait for an answer, but run to the next hut
"Raiders!"

I can hear people stirring behind me as I race through
the village. I cannot stop until I have warned Father.

Suddenly I hear a loud splintering noise behind me as
the raiders attack the gate with their axes. Then they
surge into the village, with terrible, bloodcurdling cries.

As I reach our hut, the door opens and Father comes
out brandishing his sword.

"Well done, Edric," he cries. "We're ready for them!"
Then I realise everyone is awake. There is a lot of
shouting and the clash of swords and spears. We Anglo-
Saxons may not be as big as them, but we are fierce
when we're threatened. We won't give in without a fight.

"Look after your mother and sister, Edric," calls Father
as he charges into battle. The noise is deafening now. I
turn and see other women and children huddled at the
fence, away from the fighting.

from Raiders!, *by Lynne Benton*

Powerful verbs.

Adverbs.

Powerful verb.

Powerful verbs.

Powerful verbs.

Powerful verbs.

Powerful verbs.

(**Pupil copymaster**)

Street Child

The matron closed her ice-cold hand over his and bent down towards him, her black bonnet crinkling. Her teeth were as black and twisted as the railings in the yard.

She pulled Jim along the corridor and into a huge green room, where boys sat in silence, staring at the bare walls. They all watched Jim as he was led through the room and out into another yard.

"Joseph!" the matron called, and a bent man shuffled after her. His head hung low below his shoulders like a stumpy bird's. He helped her to strip off Jim's clothes and to sluice him down with icy water from the pump. Then Jim was pulled into rough, itchy clothes, and his hair was tugged and jagged at with a blunt pair of scissors until his scalp felt as if it had been torn into pieces. He let it all happen to him. He was too frightened to resist. All he wanted was to be with his mother.

from Street Child, *by Berlie Doherty*

(Pupil copymaster)

Extracts about characters

Highlight the adjectives and adjectival phrases. Make notes in your book about what the highlighted words tell you about the character.

He wasn't an ogre, of course. Just a tall, thin, cross man with a loud voice, pale, staring pop-eyes, and tufts of spiky hair sticking out from each nostril. Councillor Samuel Isaac Evans was a ...

from Carrie's War, *by Nina Bawden*

There were hundreds and hundreds of people in the room, all sitting at long tables, all eating in silence. The only sound was the scraping of the knives and forks and the noise of chewing and gulping. All the benches faced the same way. Mr Sissons stood on a raised box at the end of the room, watching everyone as they waited for their food.

from Street Child, *by Berlie Doherty*

(**Pupil copymaster**)

Descriptive names

1. Read the character descriptions.
2. Draw a line to join the description to the name you think is most suitable.
3. Highlight the things in the description that helped you to decide on the correct name.
4. Write a description for the name that you haven't matched up.

The headmaster stood as still as a building at the front of the hall. He stared icily at the silent children.	**Joy Jollysmith**
His job was to make sure all the other Tinners had their candles.	**Slugger Smith**
She skipped happily to school. As usual she had a big smile pinned to her face and her eyes sparkled like diamonds.	**Mrs Goody**
	Hot Hat Jack
He was a big man with hands the size of dinner plates and a bent nose.	**Mr Stonehouse**

(**Pupil copymaster**)

Not Always a Perfect Place

"Whatever is that?"

I peered over to where she was pointing. It looked like a pile of rags.

"It's moving," whispered Beatrice.

Then I realised what it was. It was a boy scrambling to his feet. I'd seen poor people before, of course, but never so thin. Never so dirty. And never so near.

He stepped back, shielding his face with his hands.

"Don't hit me. I ain't done nothing."

"We're not going to hurt you, I promise," I said.

Beatrice made a grab at my arm. "Come away, Olivia. He's crawling with lice. He's probably got cholera, too."

I ignored her and stepped nearer to the boy. Beatrice was right. He was filthy and he smelt disgusting, but the thing that really drew my eye was a cut across his cheek. It was very deep, and in the shape of a cross, like an ugly red kiss on the side of his face.

"What happened?" I asked. "Who hurt you like this?"

The boy coughed, and the harsh sound seemed to rip through his whole body, "Old Soames, the overseer at the match factory where I work. He got the belt out and whipped me this morning."

Beatrice interrupted him. "He must have had a reason for beating you."

He turned to look at her. "He hit me because I fell, Miss. Old Soames doesn't like anyone fainting, or getting sick. But the factory fumes get in my throat and in my chest, and make me feel dizzy and sick." He coughed again. Please don't tell anyone about me. I'll never go back to that factory. I'll find other work. I'll work hard. And I'll make a better life for myself somehow."

"Send him away," Beatrice whispered to me. "Give him a chance to go. He must be crawling with fleas. The maid will have to wash the path down once he's gone."

"But it seems so cruel not to help him," I whispered back. I turned again to the boy. "How old are you?"

The boy shrugged. "Don't know. I can't count numbers and things."

Beatrice sniffed in disgust. "Then you should go to school and learn."

"Schools cost money. We ain't got none."

"Well, you were fortunate to have a job in the factory. People like you don't know when you're well off."

"Don't be so heartless, Beatrice," I said. "Does that man beat you often?" I asked the boy.

from Not Always a Perfect Place, *by Judy Waite*

(Exemplar material)

Example of a completed planning frame

A plan for a character to be used in a story set in World War Two

- Type: an evacuee

- Speaks: quietly, whispers, stammers

- Appearance: small, boy, 6 years old, carrying gas mask, short trousers, label, eyes glistening with tears, big blue eyes, beautiful eyelashes, pale face, blond hair

- Feelings: scared, homesick, worried

- Moves: shuffles, silently, sadly (head down), stays close to sister

- Name: Peter Pocket

(Exemplar material)

Checklist and model for writing character sketches

Example of a checklist for writing character sketches ①

Structure (how the text is put together)

- Show how they are feeling through the way they move or speak

- Include special details about appearance

- Invent interesting names

- Use speech and action effectively

- Could start with a particular character type

Language (the kind/style of words used)

- Use powerful verbs

- Use adverbs

- Use adjectives

- Use alliteration

Example of modelled writing for turning plans into character sketches ②

Poppy wondered if anyone would like the look of them enough to choose them. She looked at her brother. He was a small boy with a snub nose and blond hair. He had long eyelashes that curled against his cheek. Their mum had often joked that he was too pretty for a boy! But today his face was pale and tear-stained and he sat silently staring at the ground. "Don't leave me, will you?" Peter pleaded, pressing his grubby hand into Poppy's.

Classworks Literacy Year 4 © Sue Plechowicz, Nelson Thornes Ltd 2003

Marking ladder

Name: _____

Pupil	Objective	Teacher
	I showed my character's feelings in my sketch by using powerful verbs and adverbs.	
	I used a few special details about appearance.	
	I avoided unnecessary details.	
	I gave him/her an interesting name, possibly using alliteration.	
	I showed more about my character by what he/she says and does.	
	What could I do to improve my character sketch next time?	

Persuasive Writing

Outcome

A persuasive letter to the head teacher on a school-related issue; an advertisement or poster persuading other children to read more books

---

Objectives

Sentence

3 to understand how the grammar of a sentence alters when the sentence type is altered, when e.g. a statement is made into a question, a question becomes an order, a positive statement is made negative, noting e.g.: the order of words; verb tenses; additions and/or deletions of words; changes to punctuation.

4 to use connectives, e.g. adverbs, adverbial phrases, conjunctions, to structure an argument, e.g. 'if', 'then', 'finally', 'so'.

Text

18 to investigate how style and vocabulary are used to convince the intended reader.

19 to evaluate advertisements for their impact, appeal and honesty, focusing in particular on how information about the product is presented: exaggerated claims, tactics for grabbing attention, linguistic devices, e.g. puns, jingles, alliteration, invented words.

20 to summarise a sentence or paragraph by identifying the most important elements and rewording them in a limited number of words.

23 to present a point of view in writing, e.g. in the form of a letter, a report or a script, linking points persuasively and selecting style and vocabulary appropriate to the reader.

25 to design an advertisement, such as a poster or radio jingle on paper or screen.

Speaking and listening

● Discussion and group interaction – decide on roles for group members, identify resources needed.

ICT

● Work on presenting information to support speech.

Planning frame

● Read and analyse structural features of persuasive texts.

● Present a point of view and discuss how it is related to fact and opinion.

● The children summarise arguments.

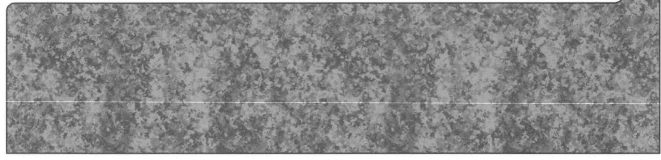

How you could plan this unit

Day 1	Day 2	Day 3	Day 4	Day 5
Reading and analysing	**Reading and analysing**	**Modelling and writing** Using writing frame (Resource Page C), the children write own opening, stating issue and opinion. Possible subjects: uniform, football in playground, tuck shop	**Writing and analysis** *Grammar for Writing* Unit 32. Identify time, cause and effect connectives in the model letter. How are they used to develop argument?	**Writing**
Structuring the Text	*Purpose and Audience*			*Using Connectives*

Day 6	Day 7	Day 8	Day 9	Day 10
Writing The children improve/edit first draft, ensuring use of emotive language, stating opinions as facts and other points from checklists	**Writing** Model how to write summary of arguments. The children write own summary	**Writing** *Grammar for Writing* Unit 31. Plenary: model changing some statements into rhetorical questions to make them more effective	**Writing** *Letter to the Head*	**Writing** Complete final draft of letter and then evaluate using marking ladder (Resource Page I)

Day 11	Day 12	Day 13	Day 14	Day 15
Reading and analysis Read a selection of advertisements and flyers. Do they use the same techniques as other persuasive texts?	**Reading and analysis** *Slogans*	**Writing** Design an advertisement, poster or flyer for a school book fair	**Writing** Complete advert, poster or flyer and evaluate using marking ladder (Resource Page J)	**Speaking and listening** In groups, the children turn persuasive text into a speech to persuade a reluctant reader to attend the book fair. One group could present their speech in assembly

17

Structuring the Text

Objective

We will look at the way persuasive texts are put together

You need: Resource Pages A–D and H.

Whole class work

- Introduce the genre of persuasive writing and record on a genre card. *What do we mean by 'persuasive' or 'to persuade'? How would you persuade someone to do (or not do) something, or to buy an item or service?*

- Brainstorm different types of persuasive text:

> health care leaflets or books – giving up smoking, five portions of fruit and vegetables per day
>
> elections – people asking you to vote for them on the School Council
>
> charity leaflets – give your money, give your time
>
> advertisements – in the paper, on billboards, on TV, web sites

- Read *Calling All Sleepyheads* (Resource Page A). Brainstorm the different components, using the annotated example (Resource Page B), and develop a checklist for class use (see Resource Page H for ideas).

- Introduce the writing frame (Resource Page C) and ensure the children understand how it relates to the annotated text.

- *What is the difference between fact and opinion? Identify both in the text.*

Independent, pair or guided work

- In pairs, the children read *Being Sun Smart* (Resource Page D) and write notes on to their writing frames.

Plenary

- *Did your text fit on to the frame?*

- Point out that, as a class, you have now read different persuasive texts and that they have similar structures. *So, if you want to write a good piece of persuasive text, structuring it in this way would be helpful.*

- *Why is the summary important? What should it contain? Why should it be fairly short?*

Purpose and Audience

Objectives

We will consider the purpose and audience for our text, and the use of emotive language

You need: Resource Pages A, B, D and H; whiteboards.

Whole class work

- Review work from the previous lesson.

- *Today we are going to focus on purpose and audience.*

- *If we want to grab the reader's attention, what do we need?* Answer: effective language.

- Reread *Calling all Sleepyheads* (Resource Page A), asking the children to think about any language features the author uses to hook the reader. Brainstorm language features and record on a class checklist, using the annotated example (Resource Page B) and checklist 1 (Resource Page H) for ideas.

- Explain briefly that rhetorical questions are questions directed to the reader and that they challenge the reader to think more carefully about the issue.

- Introduce the term 'emotive language' and ask the children to discuss the following with their response partner:
  - *Can you identify any emotive language in the text?*
  - *What does it aim to make you feel?*
  - *Is it successful?*

- Remind the children about fact and opinion and challenge them to write a fact about sleep on their whiteboards. Share ideas.

Independent, pair or guided work

- In pairs, the children identify the language features used in *Being Sun Smart* (Resource Page D). Because you have covered so many features in the shared part of this lesson, the children could be given a support sheet of questions for this activity.

Plenary

- *Did your text have any of the same language features we found yesterday?*

- Point out again that you have read several persuasive texts and that all have some or all of the language features on the checklist. *So, if you want to write a good piece of persuasive text, using some or all of these features would help you to hook your reader.*

Using Connectives

Objective

We will use connectives to structure an argument

You need: Resource Page E; whiteboards.

Whole class work

- Referring to the class checklist and the model letter about homework (Resource Page E), model writing two key points on the homework issue.

> When you do homework, you have to find the answers for yourself.
>
> I like to show my parents what we're doing at school.

- Focus on cause and effect connectives: 'because', 'and so', 'thus'. Brainstorm some others.

- Model using connectives to write a persuasive sentence:

> Finally, it is important that children do homework, because ...

Independent, pair or guided work

- Ask the children to think about the homework issue and to write one argument on their whiteboards using a cause and effect connective.

- Check that each child has written a suitable argument and used a connective correctly.

- Explain that they should copy this argument on to their writing frame and then try out another one on their whiteboard, using different language features.

- The children repeat this exercise in drafting/editing until they have completed their main body of text.

Plenary

- Share some work and ask the children to evaluate using a response sandwich: one good comment, followed by an idea on how to improve the work, followed by a second good comment.

- *Is that a successful argument? Is it fact or opinion?*

Letter to the Head

Objectives

We will write a letter about a school-related issue, presenting our point of view, linking points persuasively and using a style and vocabulary appropriate to the reader

You need: Resource Page E.

Whole class work

- Model writing the first few lines of your persuasive text into a letter (refer to Resource Page E).

- Demonstrate how a letter is more personal because you know exactly who the reader/audience is, that is, the person to whom you are writing it.

- Show your class how the structure of the text lends itself to the paragraph breaks in the letter.

- *Why is it important to include questions that need a reply?* Answer: to prompt the reader to take action – to do something.

Independent, pair or guided work

- Brainstorm some school 'issues'. Make sure the children know what is appropriate and inappropriate, for example, no personal criticisms of teachers. Focus on issues such as uniform, the school council, Sports Day, fundraising days, homework, using the Internet and so on.

- The children write a plan for a persuasive letter to the head teacher expressing their point of view on a chosen issue.

- Review using connectives to demonstrate cause and effect.

- The children draft their letters, using computers where possible.

Plenary

- Share some examples and after each one ask: *Do you think this will persuade the reader? What else could be added to make it even more persuasive?*

- Select children to read their letters with expression and emphasis.

Slogans

Objectives

We will identify the linguistic and other features used in slogans

You need: Resource Pages F and G.

Whole class work

- Display Resource Page F, concealing annotations. Ask the children to identify any features of persuasive writing that they notice in the text.

- Remind the children that puns are a type of wordplay involving words that sound the same or similar, or have more than one meaning.

- Brainstorm some more examples of wordplay in popular advertising.

Independent, pair or guided work

- Identify the features used in the list of slogans for books (Resource Page G):

  > not full sentences
  >
  > use of humour
  >
  > use of rhyme
  >
  > alliteration
  >
  > use of question and answer: books/reading solve a problem

- *Which do you think are the most effective? Why?*

- *Which might be most effective for adults/children?*

- *Can you think of any more slogans or examples of wordplay to persuade people to read more?*

- The children write some of their own slogans for reading.

Plenary

- Discuss some of the slogans added by the children.

- *Which is the shortest? Which is the longest? Which is the funniest? Which is the most effective? Which is the cleverest?*

- The children vote thumbs up or thumbs down for the best slogan.

Calling All Sleepyheads

Sleep is important. Nobody fully understands why we need sleep, but scientists think that the body uses the time to recover and to repair damage. When we fall asleep our heart and breathing rates slow down, muscles relax and our senses rest. If this is the case, are you giving your body enough rest?

Lack of sleep means that the body and the brain do not work properly. If you don't go to bed at a reasonable time, you will be sleepy in class and not learn so much. Tiredness means you may not be able to think clearly, and you may also be a danger to other people. Accidents can happen. You will lack energy, and even playing becomes too much of an effort. Is staying up late really worth it?

There is some truth in the old saying 'Early to bed and early to rise, makes us healthy, wealthy and wise.' Next time you start to argue about your bedtime, remember your body needs a break.

Give it a rest.

from Have Your Say *by Karavis and Matthews*

Classworks Literacy Year 4 © Sue Plechowicz, Nelson Thornes Ltd 2003

(Exemplar analysis)

Example of analysis of *Calling All Sleepyheads*

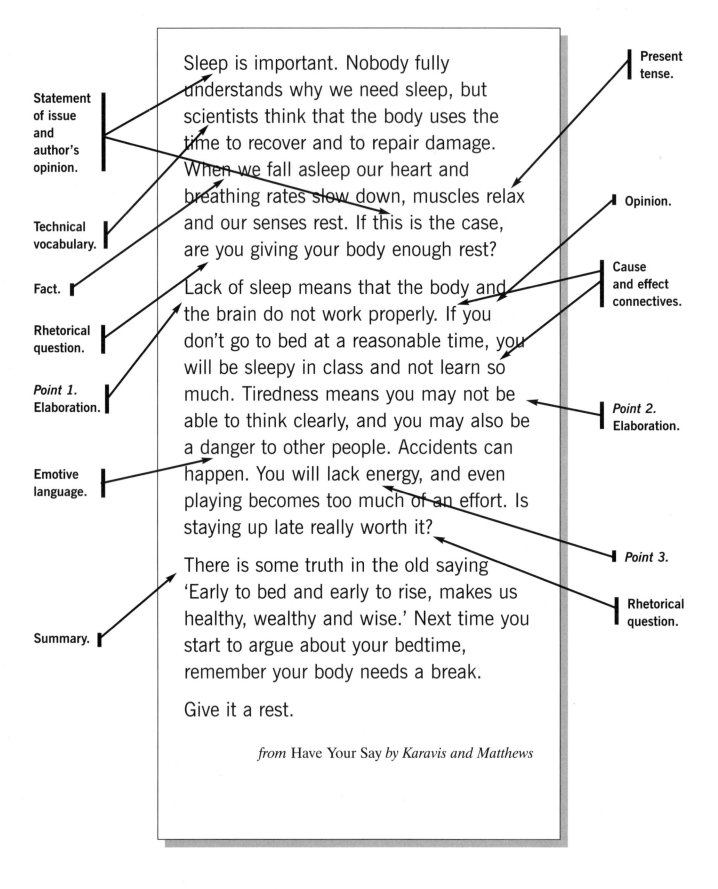

Statement of issue and author's opinion.

Technical vocabulary.

Fact.

Rhetorical question.

Point 1. **Elaboration.**

Emotive language.

Summary.

Sleep is important. Nobody fully understands why we need sleep, but scientists think that the body uses the time to recover and to repair damage. When we fall asleep our heart and breathing rates slow down, muscles relax and our senses rest. If this is the case, are you giving your body enough rest?

Lack of sleep means that the body and the brain do not work properly. If you don't go to bed at a reasonable time, you will be sleepy in class and not learn so much. Tiredness means you may not be able to think clearly, and you may also be a danger to other people. Accidents can happen. You will lack energy, and even playing becomes too much of an effort. Is staying up late really worth it?

There is some truth in the old saying 'Early to bed and early to rise, makes us healthy, wealthy and wise.' Next time you start to argue about your bedtime, remember your body needs a break.

Give it a rest.

from Have Your Say *by Karavis and Matthews*

Present tense.

Opinion.

Cause and effect connectives.

Point 2. **Elaboration.**

Point 3.

Rhetorical question.

(**Pupil copymaster**)

Persuasive text writing frame

Title:

Issue:

Author's opinion:

1st point:
Elaboration:

2nd point:
Elaboration:

3rd point:
Elaboration:

4th point:
Elaboration:

5th point:
Elaboration:

Summary of arguments:

Being Sun Smart

Safe in the sun

It is very important to take care in the sun. Young skin is very delicate and damage can sometimes be permanent and cause serious problems later in life.

Heatstroke

Too much sun on the head or back of the neck can cause headaches, nausea and faintness. Some people can get heat rash or 'prickly heat'. By following simple guidelines you can still enjoy the sunshine.

Avoid the midday sun

UV light is strongest in the summer between 11am and 3pm. Avoid staying out in the sun in the middle of the day.

Spend time in the shade

You can play in the shade, under trees or beach umbrellas to avoid getting too hot.

Cover up

Wear a wide-brimmed sun hat to protect your head and neck or a legionnaire's peaked cap with flap over the neck. Loose clothes will help you stay cool.

Always use sunscreen

Choose the sun protection factor (SPF) for your skin type, and rub in the sunscreen carefully on all areas of the skin that are exposed to the sun. Dermatologists (skin doctors) recommend that children should always use a high protection factor, at least SPF15. Re-apply your sunscreen generously at regular intervals, especially after playing in water. Water reflects the sun's rays, intensifying their effect, so for long outdoor exposure, wear a long-sleeved T-shirt.

Drink plenty

When you are hot, you sweat and lose water so you need to replace it. In order to do this, you need to drink plenty so you don't get dehydrated (too dry).

Be Sun Smart!

Classworks Literacy Year 4 © Sue Plechowicz, Nelson Thornes Ltd 2003

(Pupil copymaster)

Model letter about homework

Dear ....

<u>As you know</u> the question of whether primary school children should have to do homework has probably been discussed ever since children started attending schools. Teachers, parents, politicians and, of course, children have always had their opinion about it. At last, the Government has decided that all primary children must do some homework every night. This is very helpful because now there can be no excuses! <u>I'm sure you will agree that</u> homework is an important form of learning. If children have to go home and find out information in encyclopaedias or on the Internet, then they learn a lot more than they could by just being given the facts by their teachers. For instance, they may be looking up a fact about Martin Luther King but will also be practising ICT skills if they are using their computer or general research skills if they are using books. It would be unkind not to let children benefit from this extra practise. Secondly, homework is good for family life because children enjoy sharing their schoolwork and it gives parents a chance to show that they think schoolwork is important. What child wouldn't want to show their parents how much they know? Further more, parents have more time to help children with any problems they may have.

Although children do need to spend some spare time playing in the fresh air, homework is a good activity with which to fill in any extra spare time. Chris Davis, the chairman of the National Association for Primary Education wrote in the *Times* in 1995, that 'Children do need time to switch off as well, but most of us agree they spend far too much time in front of the television.' <u>Do you think he is correct?</u> <u>Certainly</u>, in 2002, experts say that children also spend too much time playing computer games.
Finally, it is important to get primary children used to having to do homework because when they go to secondary school they have to do it. It is a fact that children would find secondary school homework very hard if they hadn't practised doing it when they were younger. <u>We need to help our children settle quickly into their next school, don't we?</u>

Homework helps children learn more, helps family life, helps keep children occupied and helps them cope with secondary school life. The plain fact is <u>we need to make sure homework is set for every child in our class</u>.

Homework Helps!

Yours sincerely,

(Exemplar analysis)

Example of analysis of *Slogans and wordplay*

Alliteration.

Language youngsters would use so suggesting that it's trendy. Also implies that it is faster than any other skateboard.

Question to reader daring reader to disagree.

Wordplay. Name suggests you will be a winner.

Rhyme and pattern.

Alliteration.

Pun (glass is transparent, lets light in).

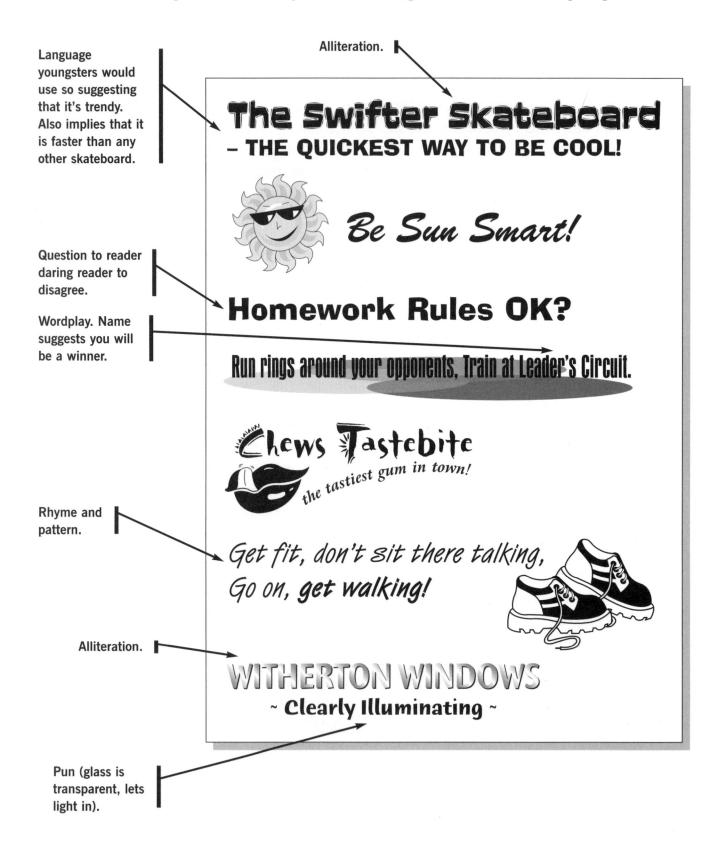

The Swifter Skateboard
– THE QUICKEST WAY TO BE COOL!

Be Sun Smart!

Homework Rules OK?

Run rings around your opponents, Train at Leader's Circuit.

Chews Tastebite
the tastiest gum in town!

Get fit, don't sit there talking,
Go on, get walking!

WITHERTON WINDOWS
~ Clearly Illuminating ~

Slogans for books

While away the ages, turn the pages!

Books take you to another world.

Need to relax? Lose yourself in a book.

Growing bored? Get a book.

In need of adventure? *Read a book.*

BOOKS BEAT BOREDOM.

Get hooked on books.

Books Rule OK?

(Exemplar material)

Checklists for persuasive writing

Example of a checklist for persuasive writing ①

Structure

- Open with a statement of the issue being addressed

- State your position on the issue

- Main body of text contains arguments that are elaborated with reasons and evidence (facts)

- End with a summary

Language features

- Use mainly the present tense

- Use logical and cause and effect connectives

- Use emotive language

- Use technical language

- Use rhetorical questions

- Dare the reader to disagree

- Try to make opinions sound like facts

- Use powerful verbs and strong adjectives

Example of a checklist for an advert, poster or flyer ②

- Writing should start with a question to draw reader in

- Object being advertised should be placed in the centre

- There should be a concluding statement at the end

- Writing should hook the reader further by using:
  - slogans and wordplay instead of sentences
  - alliteration
  - repetition
  - rhyme
  - strong punctuation!

- Layout should attract attention by the use of:
  - different fonts
  - different colours
  - different sizes

Classworks Literacy Year 4 © Sue Plechowicz, Nelson Thornes Ltd 2003

(Marking ladder)

Marking ladder for persuasive text

Name: _____

Pupil	Objective	Teacher
	I started by stating the issue and my opinion of it.	
	I supported my arguments with reasons and factual evidence.	
	I used time connectives to link arguments in paragraphs.	
	I summarised my arguments.	
	I used some/all of the following persuasive devices: • emotive language • rhetorical questions • cause and effect connectives • daring the reader to disagree • making my opinions sound like facts.	
	How could I improve my writing next time?	

(**Marking ladder**)

Marking ladder for an advert, flyer or poster

Name: _____

Pupil	Objective	Teacher
	I started with a question.	
	I placed the object or event being advertised in the centre.	
	I put a concluding statement at the end.	
	I tried to persuade my reader by using: • slogans and wordplay • alliteration • repetition and rhyme.	
	I grabbed attention by using different fonts, sizes and colours.	
	How could I improve my work next time?	

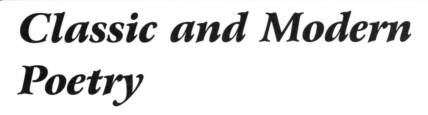

Classic and Modern Poetry

Outcome

Poems written in the style of those read; performance of own and others' poems

Objectives

Sentence
1 to revise and extend work on adjectives from Year 3 term 2 and link to work on expressive and figurative language in stories and poetry: constructing adverbial phrases; comparing adjectives on a scale of intensity.

Text
4 to understand how the use of expressive and descriptive language can e.g. create moods, arouse expectations and build tension, describe attitudes or emotions.

6 to identify clues which suggest poems are older, e.g. language use, vocabulary, archaic words.

7 to identify different patterns of rhyme and verse in poetry, e.g. choruses, rhyming couplets, alternate rhyme lines and to read these aloud effectively.

11 to write poetry based on the structure and/or style of poems read, e.g. taking account of vocabulary, archaic expressions, patterns of rhyme, choruses, similes.

Planning frame

● Read and analyse features of classic and modern poetry.

● The children write own rhyming poem and perform.

How you could plan this unit

Day 1	Day 2	Day 3	Day 4	Day 5
Reading	**Reading and analysis** Modern poetry. *The Day's Eye* and *The Poet's Brainstorm* (Resource Pages B and C)	**Writing**	**Reading** Choral reading from, for example, *Pied Piper of Hamelin*, then improving first draft	**Speaking and listening**
Old-fashioned Language		*Using Similes*		*Reading Aloud*

Day 6	Day 7	Day 8	Day 9	Day 10
Reading and writing	**Reading** Identify rhyme and rhythm pattern by counting syllables (see Resource Page H). Collect onomatopoeia words	**Reading and writing**	**Writing** Discuss alternative words for 'got' and 'then'. Place them on line of intensity. The children evaluate poems using marking ladder (Resource Page I)	**Speaking and listening** Celebration/performance. Read poems to audience
'Journey' Poems		*'Sensible' Rhymes*		

Old-fashioned Language

Objectives

We will learn how to tell if a poem is old or new. We will also think about choosing the best words for a poem

You need: Resource Pages A and H; whiteboards; Robert Louis Stevenson poem *The Moon* on a word processor (see Resource Page H).

Whole class work

- Discuss the word 'nice' (uninteresting, moderately non-committal) and brainstorm some alternatives.

- Discuss how some words become old-fashioned, for example, 'trendy'. Ask the children for other examples and mention some archaic examples: 'hastens', 'ostler'. **Why aren't these words used much now?** Answer: we have faster transport and few people use horses to travel.

- Ask the children to listen out for other archaic words as you read. Read *The Tide Rises, The Tide Falls* (Resource Page A), asking the children to close their eyes and visualise the scene. Encourage the children to tell you what picture the author has painted in their head.

- Discuss archaic words, pointing out that they are an indication that the poem was written long ago.

- Introduce the genre by telling the children about 'classic' poetry.

- Ask the children to write the poem's rhyme pattern on their whiteboards.

- Use response partners to talk about the effect of the last line of each verse. (Its rhythm is like the sea.)

- Discuss the poem's features and start a class checklist for classic poems, based on structure and language features: adjectives, alliteration, powerful verbs, repetition, and so on (see Resource Page H for ideas).

Independent, pair or guided work

- In pairs, the children read and identify features of classic poems, for example rhyme pattern, archaic words, powerful verbs.

- Introduce the term 'personification' and encourage the children to make up other examples.

- One pair works on the computer, changing the font colour of any archaic words and other features in Robert Louis Stevenson's poem *The Moon* (Resource Page H). For example, they could colour powerful verbs in red, alliteration in yellow, highlight rhyming pairs in blue and green.

Plenary

- ***What features did you find?*** Add any new ones (personification, similes and so on) to the checklist.

- Brainstorm as many words as possible that we rarely use, for example, 'frock', 'wireless' and so on. Collect these into a spelling log.

Using Similes

Objectives

We will revise work on adjectives and similes and use it to write a poem based on one we have read

You need: Resource Pages B and C; large picture of the moon.

Whole class work

- Read *The Day's Eye* (Resource Page B). *Close your eyes and try to visualise the scene. What picture does it paint in your head?*

- Establish with the class that it is a modern poem, for example, the rhyme pattern, use of adjective, alliteration, powerful verbs, repetition.

- Use response partners to discuss deeper meanings, for example:
  - *How can the sun 'surprise' the night?*
  - *What is the sudden joke?*
  - *Why is the mouth 'closing'?*

- Focus on similes. Explain that they add power to writing by creating pictures, making the reader look and think about the subject in new ways. Help the children to spell 'simile' by pointing out that it is 'smile' with an extra eye/i.

- Look at *The Poet's Brainstorm* (Resource Page C) and the ideas within it.

- Focus on a large picture of the moon with your class and brainstorm a list of adjectives/similes that might describe the moon. Encourage them to think of round things.

- Use the similes to model writing a poem for the moon. Include features from the checklist – alliteration, personification, and so on – pointing them out as you use them. Show how you amend and improve by 'thinking aloud' and continually rehearse/rewrite what you have written.

> The moon is like a pebble in the sea of stars.
> The moon is like a <u>polished</u> pebble in the sea of stars.
>
> A full stop on the blackboard of night school.
> A <u>glimmering, silver</u> full stop on the blackboard of night school.
>
> The moon is like a yawn on the face of night.
>
> The moon is like the dot on the eye of the night.

Independent, pair or guided work

- The children write a poem about the moon using similes. Some children can be guided to start their poem with the phrase: 'The moon is like …'.

- Some children can be extended by asking them to write about a crescent moon. Encourage the children to do their own brainstorm first.

Plenary

- Share some of the children's poems. Use a response sandwich to guide the evaluations: one good thing, one idea for improvement, a second good thing.

Reading Aloud

Objectives

We will identify different patterns of rhyme and verse. We will also perform a choral poem as a group

You need: Resource Pages D and E; whiteboards.

Whole class work

- Read the two poems on Resource Pages D and E. Ask the children to compare them. (They are both prayer-like.)

- Explain that *Before the Hunt* is from Nigeria. Discuss the poem:
  - *What sort of place do you think it might be?*
  - *What evidence is there in the poem to support this?*
  - *What do you like about the poem?*
  - *Which lines/phrases do you find the most effective or emotive? Why?*
  - *Why do you think the poet chose to write about this subject?*

- Point out the words 'chilling' and 'cooling' in the poem. Elicit the related adjectives ('chilly' and 'cool').

- Use have-a-go writing to brainstorm adjectives that describe heat.

- Using the children's answers, and allocating one word per child, ask the children to arrange themselves in a human line of intensity ranging from extreme cold to extreme heat. Ask two children to check the order of the rest of the class.

Independent, pair or guided work

- In mixed ability groups, prepare a choral reading of *Before the Hunt* or *The Circle of Days*. Experiment with different speeds, expression, intonation, accent and so on.

Plenary

- Each group performs to the rest of the class. ***Why did you choose that style of reading?***

- Compare and contrast styles and the reasons for the differences or similarities.

'Journey' Poems

Objective

We will write a journey poem based on one we have read

You need: Resource Pages E, F and H.

Whole class work

- Reread *Before the Hunt* (Resource Page E).

- Discuss structure and identify features. Relate to checklist 1 (Resource Page H).

- Using the structure of the poem as a framework, brainstorm a plan focusing on the 'journey' the poem follows: sky and wind, earth, people and animals – the poem follows a route or map.

- Then model writing your own poem *Before the Shopping Trip* (Resource Page F). When modelling, ensure that you use other features from the checklist.

- Demonstrate how to amend and improve by 'thinking aloud' and continually edit/rewrite what you have written.

Independent, pair or guided work

- Brainstorm ideas for a poem where you have to ask for 'good luck'. Possible topics might include: sporting activities, exams, artistic performances, first day at school.

- The children write a prayer-like poem based on the structure of *Before the Hunt*.

Plenary

- Share some poems using the response sandwich for evaluation: one good thing, one idea for improvement, a second good thing.

- *Did the poem go on a 'journey'?*

'Sensible' Rhymes

Objective

We will write a rhyming poem based on one we have read

You need: Resource Pages G and H.

Whole class work

- Read and enjoy *The Troll* (Resource Page G), ensuring that the children can identify and understand the rhythm: (8, 6, 8, 7, 8, 7, 8, 7 ...)

- Model writing a poem using the same style (rhythm and rhyme patterns) and framework (see example 2, Resource Page H). Demonstrate how to ensure the choice of rhyme makes sense ('sensible' rhyme), and how to add adjectives or adverbs at the checking stage if a line doesn't have enough syllables.

FINDING RHYMING WORDS

Each time you write a line, note whether it will need to rhyme with a later one.

If so, immediately make a list of possible words.

If you can't think of many rhymes then it is not a good word to use so change the line.

If there are lots of rhymes, highlight the ones that seem appropriate for the subject and don't be tempted to use inappropriate ones.

This will ensure that the poem makes sense and the rhymes aren't forced.

Independent, pair or guided work

- Brainstorm ideas for a poem based on *The Troll*. Encourage the children to think of other fantastic characters, for example, Gollum from *The Hobbit*, or generic mythical beasts – good or bad.

- The children write a poem based on *The Troll*, with particular focus on rhythm and rhyme.

Plenary

- Read some of the poems to the class and use a response sandwich to guide the evaluations: one good thing, one idea for improvement, a second good thing.

- *Were the rhymes 'sensible'?*

- *What were the easiest words to find rhymes for? Answer:* one-syllable words.

(**Pupil copymaster**)

The Tide Rises, The Tide Falls

The tide rises, the tide falls,
The twilight darkens, the curlew calls;
Along the sea-sands damp and brown,
The traveller hastens toward the land,
And the tide rises, the tide falls.

Darkness settles on roof and walls,
But the sea, the sea in the darkness calls;
The little waves, with their soft white hands,
Efface the footprints in the sands,
And the tide rises, the tide falls.
The morning breaks; the steeds in their stalls
Stamp and neigh, as the ostler calls;
The day returns but nevermore,
Returns the traveller to the shore,
And the tide rises, the tide falls.

Henry Wadsworth Longfellow

Pupil copymaster

The Day's Eye

1. The sun rises,
surprises the weary night
like a sudden joke.
Daylight.

2. The sun gleams,
beams kindly heat
like an oven's plate.
Streets sweat.

3. The sun sneaks,
peeks through misty cloud,
like a sly thief,
alone in the crowd.

4. The sun sleeps,
creeps into cool shade
like a honey cat.
Shadows fade.

5. The sun slips,
dips into night
like a closing mouth,
swallowing light.

Pie Corbett

The Poet's Brainstorm

a cat's face looking at me

a mouth saying 'no'

a treetop

a wheel

looks like an eye

scarlet blood

gold

Sun

a hole

crimson

a round TV

round hole

red

a bus

a button

circular

Classworks Literacy Year 4 © Sue Plechowicz, Nelson Thornes Ltd 2003

The Circle of Days

(based on *Canticle of the Sun*, by Saint Francis of Assisi)

Lord, we offer you our thanks and praise
For the circle of the days.
Praise for radiant brother sun,
Who makes the hours around us run.

For sister moon, and for the stars,
Brilliant, precious, always ours.
Praise for brothers wind and air,
Serene or cloudy, foul or fair.

For sister water, clear and chaste,
Useful, humble, good to taste.
For fire, our brother, strong and bright,
Whose joy illuminates the night.

Praise for our sister, mother earth,
Who cares for each of us from birth.
For all her children, fierce or mild,
For sister, brother, parent, child.

For creatures wild, and creatures tame,
For hunter, hunted, both the same.
For brother sleep, and sister death,
Who tend the borders of our breath.

For desert, orchard, rock and tree,
For forest, meadow, mountain, sea,
For fruit and flower, plant and bush,
For morning robin, evening thrush.

For all your gifts, of every kind,
We offer praise with quiet mind.
Be with us, lord, and guide our ways
Around the circle of the days.

Reeve Lindbergh

Classworks Literacy Year 4 © Sue Plechowicz, Nelson Thornes Ltd 2003

Before the Hunt

Howling wind,
hear me,
Dancing trees,
hail me,
Cooling breeze,
calm me,
Guiding sky,
light my
way through the bush.
As the stars
protect the lonely moon
So may I
escape the snares
in this living forest.
As the cat
stalks its prey
So may I
be first to spy my game.
Living forest hear me
Chilling wind still my heart
Teasing shadows smile with me
Lead me to my hunt.

Lari Williams

(Pupil copymaster)

Before the Shopping Trip

Inviting vegetables,
entice me,
Fresh fruit,
find me,
Healthy options,
tempt me,
Best bargains,
guide me
towards your shelves.
As the squeaking trolley
pulls me this way and that,
So may I
Avoid the feet
of my fellow shoppers.
As the aroma of baking bread
tickles my taste buds,
So may I
not spend too much.
Splendid supermarket reward me
Cheerful assistants smile at me
Help me with my bags.

based on Before the Hunt, *by Lari Williams*

Classworks Literacy Year 4 © Sue Plechowicz, Nelson Thornes Ltd 2003

The Troll

Be wary of the loathsome troll
That slyly lies in wait
To drag you to his dingy hole
And put you on his plate.

His blood is black and boiling hot,
He gurgles ghastly groans.
He'll cook you in his dinner pot,
Your skin, your flesh, your bones.

He'll catch your arms and clutch your legs
And grind you to a pulp,
Then swallow you like scrambled eggs
gobble! gobble! gulp!

So watch your steps when you next go
Upon a pleasant stroll,
Or you might end up in the pit below
As supper for the troll.

Jack Prelutsky

(Exemplar material)

Checklist and models for poetry

Example of a checklist for writing a poem ①

Structure

- May have a rhyme or rhythm

- Rhythm is often more complicated in modern poems

- Lines of words are often repeated

Language features

- Archaic words in classic poems

- Words used for effect

- Powerful verbs and adjectives

- Alliteration

- Similes

- Personification

- Onomatopoeia

Example of modelled writing (with counted syllables) ②

I'm scared of the gruesome beast, (7)
That's waiting there for me. (6)
He wants me for a family feast, (8)
They'll eat me for their tea. (6)

His eyes are red and popping out, (8)
His teeth are sharp as pins. (6)
His fists will give me such a clout, (8)
He always, always wins. (6)

Alternative rhymes

least, feast, increased, decreased
see, fee, flee, tea, pea, key, flea, bee, tree
shout, about, clout, scout, pout, doubt
fins, dins, wins, twins, sins, begins

The Moon, by Robert Louis Stevenson ③

The Moon has a face like the clock in the hall;
She shines on thieves on the garden wall,
On streets and fields and harbour quays,
And birdies asleep in the forks of the trees.

The squalling cat and the squeaking mouse,
The howling dog by the door of the house,
The bat that lies in bed at noon,
All love to be out by the light of the moon.

But all of the things that belong to the day,
Cuddle to sleep to be out of her way;
And flowers and children close their eyes,
Till up in the morning the sun shall arise.

(**Marking ladder**)

Name: _____

Pupil	Objective	Teacher
	I copied rhythm and rhyme patterns where appropriate.	
	I used repetition for effect.	
	I used powerful verbs and adjectives.	
	I used some of the following: • alliteration • personification • onomatopoeia • similes.	
	How could I improve my poem next time?	

Narrative Writing Using Paragraphs

Outcome

A story written in paragraphs from a plan, set in World War Two (curricular links to history)

Objectives

Sentence

1 to reread own writing to check for grammatical sense (coherence) and accuracy (agreement); to identify errors and to suggest alternative constructions.

2 to revise work on verbs from Year 3 term 1 and to investigate verb tenses (past, present and future): compare sentences from narrative and information texts, e.g. narrative in past tense, explanations in present tense, forecasts/ directions in future; to develop awareness of how tense relates to purpose and structure of text; to understand the term 'tense' in relation to verbs and use it appropriately; to understand that one test of whether a word is a verb is whether or not its tense can be changed.

4 to use speech marks and other dialogue punctuation appropriately and to use the conventions which mark boundaries between spoken words and the rest of the sentence. [Year 3 objective]

5 to practise using commas to mark grammatical boundaries within sentences; link to work on editing and revising own writing.

Text

1 to investigate how settings are built up from small details, and how the reader responds to them.

3 to explore chronology in narrative using written or other media texts, by mapping how much time passes in the course of the story, e.g. noticing where there are jumps in time, or where some events are skimmed over quickly, and others told in detail.

4 to explore narrative order, identify and map out the main stages of the story: introductions → build-ups → climaxes or conflicts → resolutions.

9 to use different ways of planning stories e.g. using brainstorming, notes, diagrams.

10 to plan a story identifying the stages of its telling.

12 to write independently, linking own experience to situations in historical stories, e.g., How would I have responded? What would I do next?

15 to use paragraphs in story writing to organise and sequence the narrative.

Speaking and listening

● telling and retelling stories; using different story-telling techniques; discussing how telling is adapted to audience.

Planning frame

● Understand the stages in developing narrative. Identify: introduction, build-up, climax, resolution and ending.

- Practise telling a story from a plan.

- Investigate verb tenses and how the tense relates to the purpose and structure of the text.

- Practise using commas to mark grammatical boundaries and ensure use in own stories.

- The children write their own story.

Note

- It is helpful if this unit is preceded by work on character sketches (see page 1).

- You will need a copy of *The Enemy Airman*, by Dennis Hamley (Rigby Navigator).

How you could plan this unit

Day 1	Day 2	Day 3	Day 4	Day 5
Reading and writing Introduce genre and purpose (to entertain and help us feel what it was like to live in other times). Read *The Enemy Airman*. Discuss a possible plan. The children plan own story using Resource Page A	**Writing** *Story Hills*	**Planning, speaking and listening** Draw a storyboard for *The Enemy Airman*. Children draw storyboard for their own story. (Each picture indicates at least one new paragraph.) Tell own stories to partners/groups using storyboards	**Writing and analysis** *Grammar for Writing* Unit 21. Add 'past tense' to language feature checklist	**Writing** *The Introduction*

Day 6	Day 7	Day 8	Day 9	Day 10
Writing Improve first draft of introduction using checklist and write up for presentation. Ensure correct use of commas	**Writing** *The Build-up*	**Writing** Improve first draft of build-up and then write up on presentation copy or use DTP on computer	**Writing** *Dialogue*	**Modelling and writing** The children write climax of own story including dialogue from Day 9

Day 11	Day 12	Day 13	Day 14	Day 15
Modelling and writing The children improve first draft of climax and write or use computer	**Modelling and writing** The children write resolution of own story	**Reading and Writing** *Linked Endings*	**Reading and analysis** Reread Resource Page G and discuss checklists. The children improve first draft of ending and then write or use computer	**Speaking and listening** Share the stories, preferably with an audience. The children evaluate their story using the marking ladder (Resource Page J)

Story Hills

Objectives

We will look at different ways of planning a story, then we will plan our own story in stages

You need: Resource Pages B and C; a story such as *The Enemy Airman*, by Dennis Hamley (Rigby Navigator); flip chart.

Whole class work

- Remind the children that stories have a similar basic structure and that this can be represented as a story hill.

- Discuss the story hill (Resource Page B), emphasising that the 'build-up' of a story can also be used to build up small details about the characters.

- Point out that the resolution is not the end of the story. The resolution is when the problem is solved by the characters but the ending is the 'tying up' of all the details. The ending should also link back to the beginning so this has to be planned.

- Refer to a story the children are familiar with, for example *The Enemy Airman*: **How does the author link his ending with the beginning?** Answer: news of Dad.

- Ask the children to help you to put the story on to the hill. Start with the introduction, then the climax, resolution and ending.

- Reading aloud from the text, identify how the story and characters are developed. Explain that only key events and changes of setting are put on the hill.

- Discuss that events on the hill are linked to paragraphs. When writing, the author starts a new paragraph for each new idea, new setting or new person talking.

- Share the modelled example of a story hill (Resource Page C). Explain that it does not have lots of details or the ending because you want this to be a surprise.

Independent, pair or guided work

- Using the blank frame (Resource Page B), the children place their own story on to a story hill. Mention that they can change their story from yesterday's original brainstorm plan if they think they have a better idea.

- The children storyboard their work.

- With some children, you can plan a group story on a flip chart. (These children can be supported throughout the unit, working together on the group story during the planning stages, but can individualise when it comes to writing the actual story.)

Plenary

- Ask the children to rehearse the basic structure of the story:

> Characters are faced with <u>a problem</u> that <u>builds up</u> until it is so bad (<u>climax</u>) something has to be done about it. The problem is solved in some way (<u>resolution</u>) and then the <u>ending</u> ties up all other information and links back to the beginning.

- Select children to share the problem and climax in their story. (It may be too early to share the resolution and some children may wish to keep it as a surprise.)

The Introduction

Objective

We will write an introduction to our own story

You need: Resource Pages C, D and I.

Whole class work

- Explain that you are going to read the introduction of your story today.

- Review the story hill for *Who will pick the Pockets?* (Resource Page C) to ensure that the children are clear about which events make up the introduction.

- Remind the children that each event will be a new paragraph, but that you may have more than one paragraph for each event.

- Display the text (Resource Page D) and read it to the class. Invite comments.

- The children use the checklist for character sketches (see Resource Page I, checklist 2) to evaluate whether you have started to build up your characters.

- Refer to checklist 1 (language features) and point out (if the children haven't already) that the story is in the past tense. Remind them that they need to use effective language to hook their readers.

- Challenge the children to highlight effective words: powerful verbs, adverbs, strong adjectives and so on.

- Explain that it might be helpful for the children to use your story as a guide or frame for theirs. For example, they could start with:

  > The ———— family, Mum, ——— year old ————and
  > ————, ————, lived in —————

Independent, pair or guided work

- The children write the introduction to their stories, referring to the checklists and their story hills or storyboards.

Plenary

- Share a few introductions and ask the children to use a response sandwich to guide the evaluations: one good thing, one idea for improvement, a second good thing.

The Build-up

Objective

We will write the build-up for our own story

You need: Resource Pages C, E and I.

Whole class work

- Tell the children that you are going to read the build-up of your story today.

- Refer them to the story hill for *Who will pick the Pockets?* (Resource Page C) and ensure that they are clear about the events that make up this section.

- Remind the children that each event will be a new paragraph but that you may have more than one paragraph for each event.

- Display the text (Resource Page E) and read it to the class. Invite comments.

- Challenge the children to use the class checklist for character sketches to evaluate whether you have continued to build up your characters.

- The children can also refer to language features on checklist 1 (Resource Page I).

Independent, pair or guided work

- The children write the build-up part of their stories referring to the checklists and their story hills or storyboards.

Plenary

- Share some work and ask the children to use a response sandwich to guide evaluations: one good thing, one idea for improvement, a second good thing.

- *Does the story hook the reader's attention? Do we care about the characters? What do you think might happen next?*

Dialogue

Objectives

We will practise our punctuation, then write some dialogue for our story

You need: Resource Pages F and H; whiteboards.

Whole class work

- Display the unpunctuated dialogue (Resource Page H) and explain that it is the first draft of some dialogue to go into your story. The children discuss with their response partners.

- *What did you notice about this writing?* Answer: lack of punctuation and boring verbs.

- *What can I do to improve it?*

- Ask individual children to come up and punctuate the text a line at a time. *How did you know where to put that punctuation?*

- The children write on their whiteboards where the new paragraphs would be by writing down the last word of one and the first word of the next. Check by highlighting the line breaks on the board.

- Collaborate on replacing the 'saids' for powerful verbs and adding some adverbs.

Independent, pair or guided work

- Discuss how dialogue has to fit the characters in terms of: their age, the time the story is set, what mood they are in (happy, scared, cross), who they are speaking to, possibly even their accent, and so on.

- The children write dialogue to use in the climax section of their stories.

Plenary

- Read the extract from *Who will pick the Pockets?* showing the dialogue (Resource Page F).

- *Is this effective dialogue? What did you like/dislike about it? How can I improve it?*

Linked Endings

Objective

We will write an ending for our story which links to the beginning

You need: Resource Page G.

Whole class work

- Read the ending of your story (Resource Page G) and invite comments. ***Did you expect this to happen? Why did you think that? What do you think might happen next?***

- Prompt the children to notice the link to the beginning of your story. (The colour red, red doorstep, red door.)

- Remind the children that they need to write a link in their stories. Allow them time to plan a link if they have not already done so.

Independent, pair or guided work

- The children work on the ending for their own stories, referring to their planning frame to write the link between the beginning and the ending.

- The children can add a detail to their beginning during editing if they have not got a detail that can be 'linked' to the ending.

Plenary

- Share some stories. See if the 'link' can be identified, even if the children haven't heard/read the beginning.

- Ask the children to evaluate using response sandwich: one good thing, one idea for improvement, a second good thing.

- ***Which were the best 'links' or 'twists'?***

Planning frame

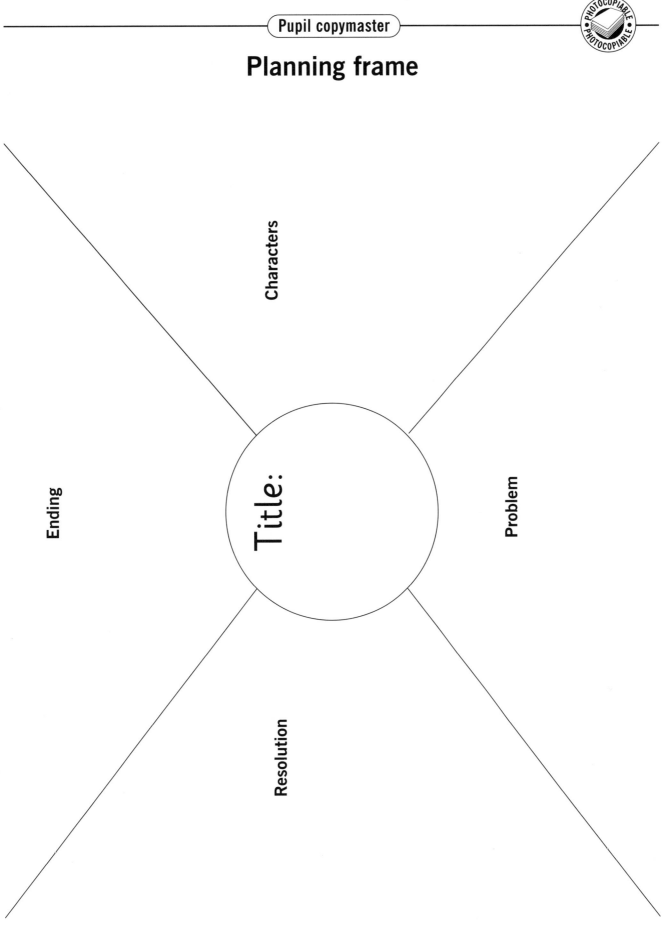

(Pupil copymaster)

Story hill

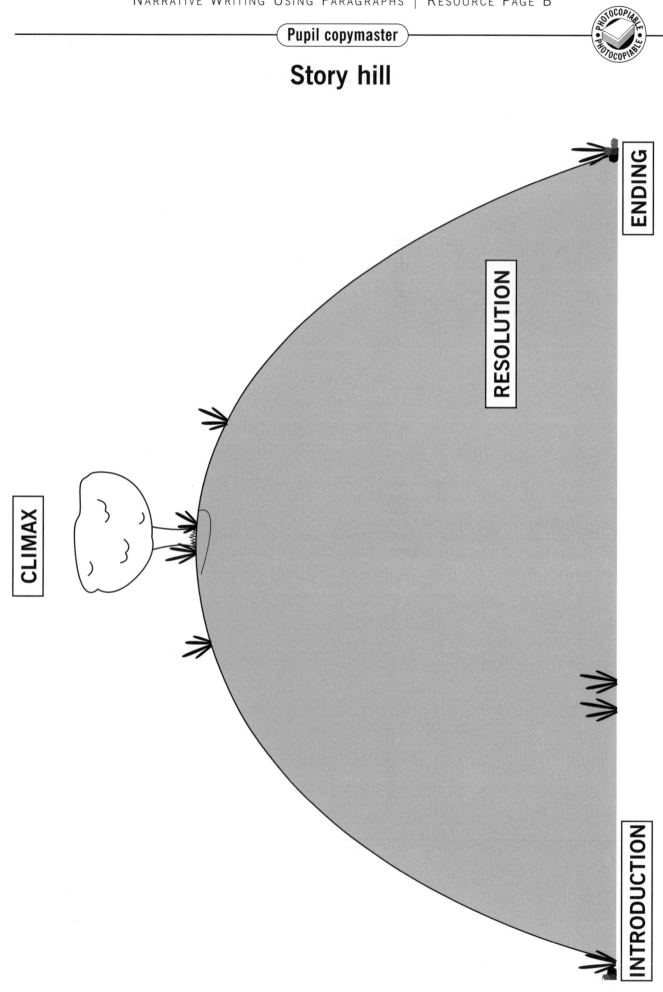

Classworks Literacy Year 4 © Sue Plechowicz, Nelson Thornes Ltd 2003

Exemplar material

Who will pick the Pockets? – story hill

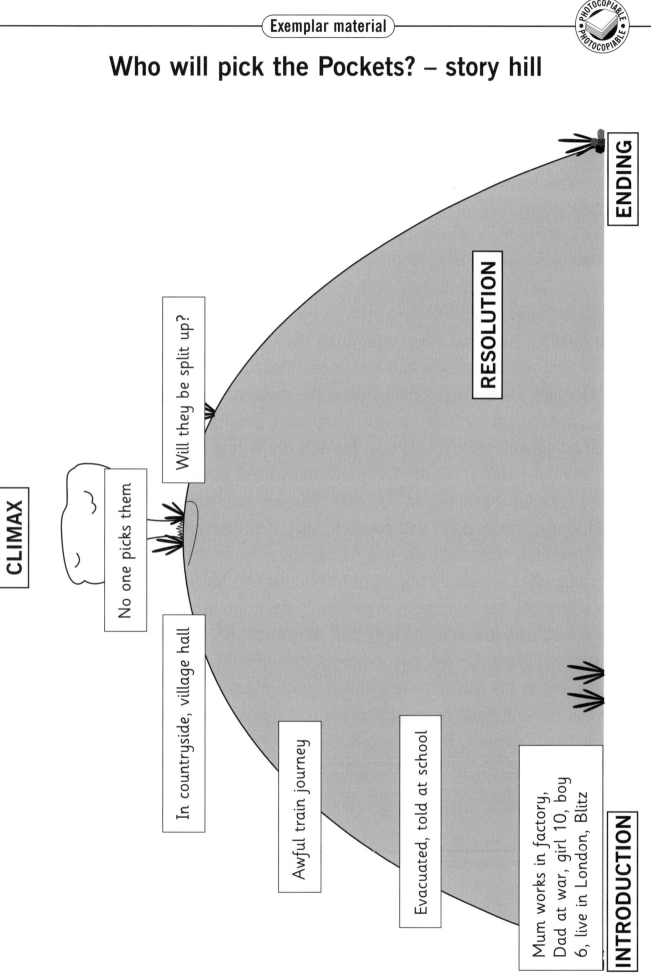

ENDING

RESOLUTION

CLIMAX

Will they be split up?

No one picks them

In countryside, village hall

Awful train journey

Evacuated, told at school

Mum works in factory, Dad at war, girl 10, boy 6, live in London, Blitz

INTRODUCTION

Classworks Literacy Year 4 © Sue Plechowicz, Nelson Thornes Ltd 2003

Who will pick the Pockets? – introduction

The Pocket family, Mum, ten-year old Poppy, and Peter, six, lived in a small terraced house in the centre of London. Mum worked hard in a factory where they made the massive, silver barrage balloons that floated silently above the city roof-tops.

Dad was away fighting in the army. Before the war he had been a postman, delivering letters to all their neighbours. Sometimes, in the school holidays Poppy was allowed to go with Dad and she was amazed to see that he often delivered much more than the letters!

"I'll just pop these eggs into Mrs Jones, Poppy," he'd say with a smile.

"Her legs are too bad for walking at the moment." Or he'd take a newspaper to old Mr Smith whose cough was playing him up again. Poppy loved going with her dad. He'd let her slip the letters into the letterboxes and call out cheerily, "Post!" She particularly liked going to Number 68, the house with the gleaming red doorstep. Dad had explained that the lady used to use special paint and polish to keep it so shiny. Poppy thought it was beautiful. "Just like you, love," Dad would tease. "Poppy red!"

Poppy often wondered how poor Mrs Jones and Mr Smith managed now and she shook her head sadly when she passed the dusty pile of rubble and one ruined wall that was the only part of Number 68 left after a really bad air raid last week. On the way to school today Poppy peered at the pile of rubble and in the sunlight she suddenly noticed one or two pieces of red-painted brick. It must be what was left of the beautiful step. A tear slid down Poppy's cheek. Today the red made her think of something else. Not paint but blood. Poppy shivered, grabbed Peter's hand and started running towards the school.

Who will pick the Pockets? – build-up

When they arrived at school Poppy and Peter stored their suitcases beneath their pegs just as they had done for the past two weeks. Poppy would never forget the day that Mum had plonked the cases onto their beds and tearfully explained that they were to pack them with one set of clothes and one special toy. "They're your evacuation cases," Mum had explained, in answer to their confused looks. "You must take them to school every day until Mr Stonehouse tells you it's your turn to go."

"Go where?" Peter demanded.

"To the countryside. You'll be evacuated to somewhere safe. Somewhere the bombers can't reach you." With that Mum turned and rushed from the room and from then on they had dutifully lugged their cases to and from school, never really believing that they would actually go anywhere. On that morning when Poppy filed into assembly with her class, Mr Stonehouse, the Headmaster, was at the front of the hall talking quietly to Miss Honeywell. This was very strange because usually Mr Stonehouse insisted on total silence. "You will be still and silent. As silent as a stone house!" he would order without even the smallest glimmer of a smile at his own joke. Even Slugger Smith in the top class didn't dare to disturb Mr Stonehouse's silence.

Something was not right. Poppy felt the hairs on the back of her neck start to prickle, she felt hot, her cheeks burned. She scanned the room for Peter. He was standing near the front. Poppy glared at the back of his neck, willing him to turn around. For some reason she wanted to see his face and his cheeky grin. Suddenly, Mr Stonehouse's stern voice echoed around the hall.

"Girls and boys, I have here a letter which tells me that today, yes today, is THE DAY." Slowly he looked around the room, making sure he had everyone's rapt attention. "Today is Evacuation Day!"

Gasps filtered around the room but Poppy stayed silent. She watched Peter's head whizz around as he searched the lines for her. When their gazes locked together, Poppy saw Peter's eyes glisten and a fat tear rolled silently down his pale face.

The next hour past in what seemed like a minute. There was a flurry of activity as teachers handed out labels and helped tie them onto everyone's coats. Poppy saw that hers had 'Poppy Pocket' and the school address on it. Then everyone was told to take their cases and their gas masks and to line up in the front playground. Some of the older children were laughing and joking but many of the younger ones were tearful. The older ones were told to find their younger brothers and sisters and to do their best to reassure them. Poppy found Peter looking very lost and scared.

"I want Mum," he wailed pitifully as soon as he saw Poppy. Poppy wanted Mum too but she knew she mustn't think about that. She had to be brave for Peter.

The whole school walked in one enormous crocodile to the train station. Occasionally someone's mother would dash along the pavement, calling to their son or daughter. When they spotted them they would hug them briefly before the crocodile continued its relentless progress. Once at the station more mothers searched up and down for the last sight of their children before they were herded aboard the waiting train, the train that was to take their children to safety but at that moment seemed only to be stealing them away to an unknown and uncertain future. Poppy looked around desperately, hoping for a glimpse of their mum even though she knew that Mrs Pocket wouldn't be there. Mum was working the morning shift at the factory today. There was no way that she would have heard that today was THE DAY.

Who will pick the Pockets? – dialogue

Once on the train Peter brightened up considerably. They had been given a brown paper bag and inside there were some biscuits, a bottle of water and most amazingly, a bar of chocolate. Poppy supposed that the grown ups who organised this evacuation business thought that a few treats would take the children's minds off what was happening to them. Certainly the thought of the unexpected feast worked a treat for Peter. No sooner had the train huffed and puffed its way out of the station than Peter started nagging Poppy to let him start on the goodies.

"I'm starving," announced Peter loudly. "When can I eat my biscuits?"

"Not yet," Poppy said wearily, "we've only just got on the train." Poppy knew that wouldn't be the end of it though and sure enough, only a few minutes later, Peter was moaning again.

"I'm really starving, my tummy is rumbling like a building collapsing!" he whined dramatically.

"Oh, go on then but don't eat them all at once." Poppy couldn't be bothered to argue with him any more. She peered out of the window, screwing up her eyes to try to stop the tears from escaping. Mum's voice echoed in her head.

"You must be brave, Poppy love. Be strong and look after Peter." Poppy knew what she had to do but it was so hard.

"It's too hard," she whispered sadly to the buildings that whizzed past the window. "It's too hard."

Classworks Literacy Year 4 © Sue Plechowicz, Nelson Thornes Ltd 2003

Who will pick the Pockets? – resolution and ending

Eventually they were the only children left in the room. Miss Bottomsleigh seemed to be on the verge of packing up and leaving when Poppy gave a quiet little cough.

"Excuse me, miss, but what about us?"

Miss Bottomsleigh looked startled and peered in their direction.

"Oh deary me, I didn't notice you there. I really do need new glasses you know. Tut, tut, what are we going to do with you two? There's no one left to take you!"

"Can we go back home then?" whispered Peter hopefully.

"Oh no dear. You must stay here with us where it's safe."

At that moment there was a great clattering as a large lady burst through the door.

"I'm so sorry! I'm very late. Couldn't start the old banger, had to get old Fred the gardener to push me off. Not easy, nearly did him in! Still I'm here now. I'm not too late am I? Now where are all the children?"

Poppy, Peter and Miss Bottomsleigh stared in amazement as this whirlwind of a woman rattled on and on hardly stopping for breath but eventually Miss Bottomsleigh managed to get a word in.

"Mrs Goody, it's so good of you to come but you've no choice I'm afraid. These two are the only ones left. You'll have to take one of these."

She pushed Poppy and Peter towards Mrs Goody with an apologetic smile.

"You can't split us up!" Poppy burst out. "We won't go with you if you do, WE WON'T!"

Peter watched his sister as her eyes blazed and bright spots of colour appeared in her cheeks. He'd seen her in a temper before but today he was glad of it. Poppy's arm whipped out around his shoulders and he staggered slightly as she pulled him closer to her.

"Oh no my dears," replied Mrs Goody. Her eyes twinkled and she didn't seem to be at all bothered about Poppy's temper. "Of course you must stay together. No problem with that. You can come home with me, there's plenty of room for you both."

Poppy breathed a sigh of relief and her grip on Peter relaxed slightly.

Mrs Goody led them outside where a large, black, ancient-looking car was waiting.

"Wow!" exclaimed Peter.

Poppy noticed that he was smiling for the first time in a long while. Perhaps things would be okay after all, thought Poppy.   And so they were. They arrived at a large house.

"Here we are, my dears. I know it won't be like being with your own parents but I'm sure we'll get on famously. Perhaps your mum will be able to visit before long. You must treat my house as your own home while you're here."

Poppy glanced at the big front door. It was bright, poppy red.

"Oh yes," she murmured, "things will be alright."

Dialogue to improve

I'm starving said Peter, when can I eat my biscuits? Not yet said Poppy, we've only just got on the train. A few minutes later, Peter was moaning again. I'm really starving, my tummy is rumbling he said. Oh, go on then but don't eat them all at once said Poppy. She remembered mum had said you must be brave and look after Peter. Poppy knew what she had to do but it was so hard. It's too hard she said.

(Exemplar material)

Checklists for narrative writing using paragraphs

Example of a checklist for writing a story ①

Structure (how the text is put together)

- Introduction
- Climax
- Resolution
- Ending – may have a twist at the end
- Paragraphs linked to events on hill or each picture on storyboard

Language (the kind/style of words used)

- Use the past tense
- Use effective dialogue
- Use powerful verbs
- Use adverbs
- Use strong adjectives

Example of a checklist for writing character sketches ②

Structure

- Show how they are feeling through the way they move or speak
- Include special details about appearance
- Invent interesting names
- Use speech and action effectively
- Could start with a particular character type

Language features

- Use powerful verbs
- Use adverbs
- Use adjectives
- Use alliteration

Classworks Literacy Year 4 © Sue Plechowicz, Nelson Thornes Ltd 2003

(**Marking ladder**)

Name: _____

Pupil	Objective	Teacher
	My story includes an introduction, build-up, climax, resolution and ending.	
	I have used paragraphs.	
	I have used the past tense.	
	I have included effective (but not unnecessary) dialogue.	
	I have used effective language including: • powerful verbs • adverbs • strong adjectives.	
	I have built up my characters using small details.	
	How could I improve my writing next time?	

Poetry on a Common Theme

Outcome

Poetry based on personal or imagined experience, linked to poems read

Objectives

Sentence

3 to identify the use of powerful verbs, e.g. 'hobbled' instead of 'went', e.g. through cloze procedure.

4 to identify adverbs and understand their functions in sentences through:

- identifying common adverbs with '-ly' suffix and discussing their impact on the meaning of sentences
- noticing where they occur in sentences and how they are used to qualify the meanings of verbs
- collecting and classifying examples of adverbs, e.g. for speed: 'swiftly', 'rapidly', 'sluggishly'; light: 'brilliantly', 'dimly' and so on
- investigating the effects of substituting adverbs in clauses or sentences, for example: 'They left the house …ly'
- using adverbs with greater discrimination in own writing.

Text

7 to compare and contrast poems on similar themes, particularly their form and language, discussing personal responses and preferences.

8 to find out more about popular authors, poets, etc. and use this information to move on to more books by favourite writers.

14 to write poems based on personal or imagined experience, linked to poems read. List brief phrases and words, experiment by trimming or extending sentences; experiment with powerful and expressive verbs.

Speaking and listening

- to discuss preferences to poems.

Planning frame

- Read poems about animals and note the different styles used by poets.
- Understand the importance of research and brainstorming.
- Use the same features and styles to support own writing.
- Express personal preferences to poems.

Note

- The theme for this unit is 'Creation' and you may wish to link it to R.E.

How you could plan this unit

Day 1	Day 2	Day 3	Day 4	Day 5
Reading and analysis	**Writing**	**Reading** Read *The Tiger*, by Satesh Dadlani, from *To Rhyme or Not to Rhyme*, Sandy Brownjohn. Identify similes. Brainstorm 'ingredients' for a swan (appearance, sound, movement, personality). Model a recipe-style poem. The children brainstorm, then write their own poem	**Reading, writing, planning** Using marking ladder (Resource Page J) the children evaluate and improve own poems. Read and give personal response. Research work of a poet (e.g. Roger McGough, Michael Rosen) or do subject-based search using the library or the Internet	**Reading and writing**
Doing Research	*Writing a Poem*			*Rhyme Banks*

Day 6	Day 7	Day 8	Day 9	Day 10
Writing Using rhyme bank made on Day 5, and *Johnny's Pockets* (Resource Page E), the children write their own poem	**Reading and analysis** Brainstorm a poem describing family members. The children write a similar poem	**Reading and writing**	**Reading, analysis, writing** 'The First Being made an anxious ant arriving angrily.' Identify word types and tense. Give each child a letter of the alphabet. They brainstorm adjectives, creatures, verbs, adverbs, to make a line for class poem	**Reading, speaking and listening** The children evaluate own poems using the marking ladder (Resource Page J) and celebrate some of their own creations by reading them to an audience
		Using Alliteration		

Doing Research

Objectives

We will identify some of the features that poets use in their writing and learn to research a subject before starting to write

You need: Resource Pages A, B and I; whiteboards; a selection of books on the solar system.

Whole class work

- Introduce topic: Poems with a common theme, for example 'Creation'.

- *We are going to focus on identifying some of the features poets use so we can build a checklist to help us when we write our own poems. We'll also consider what a poet has to do to plan before writing.*

- Without giving away the title, read *Goldfish* (Resource Page A). Ask the children to paint a picture in their head while you read. Then ask, **What is the poem about?**

- In pairs, the children identify, discuss and note on whiteboards the kind of words the poet has used: descriptive – adjectives, powerful verbs (mainly about movement).

- Point out that a poet aims to paint a picture in the reader's head. This is done by using descriptive language. Add this to the class checklist (see Resource Page I for ideas).

- Read *Night Fishing* (Resource Page A). **What subjects do you think the poet researched before writing this poem?** Answer: the night sky and fish.

- Collaborate on what the brainstorm might have been like.

- *If you were going to write a similar poem entitled, 'If the planets were animals', what would you need to research?* Answer: the planet plus appropriate animals.

- Tell the children that you have researched and brainstormed around the moon. Show them your sheet (Resource Page B).

Independent, pair or guided work

- Using books about the solar system and a similar planning frame, ask the children to research a given planet (or the sun).

- List key facts that the children need to establish: size, colour, temperature.

- The children choose an appropriate animal to compare it with and brainstorm how that animal moves. This is recorded on the planning frame as shown.

Plenary

- Share some children's work and evaluate using a response sandwich: one good comment, one idea for improvement, a second good idea.

- *What did you learn about that planet? Why did you choose that animal to represent it?*

Writing a Poem

Objective

We will write a poem in the style of *Night Fishing*, experimenting with powerful and expressive verbs

You need: Resource Pages A–C and I.

Whole class work

- Show the children a copy of your planning frame about the moon (Resource Page B). Ask them to identify alliteration, powerful verbs, similes and so on.

- Reread *Night Fishing* (Resource Page A) and explain that we can use a poet's work as a planning frame or model for our own poem in the same style.

- Model how to use the poem as a frame for your own poem, based on information from your plan (see example 2, Resource Page I).

- While modelling, verbalise that you are also referring to the language features on the checklist (Resource Page N): alliteration, powerful verbs and so on.

- Now read *The Sun* (Resource Page C). *In this poem the writer compares the sun to a spider. Why do you think she chose this animal? Do you think it is a successful simile? What other attributes of spiders could she have used?*

Independent, pair or guided work

- The children write their own poem using the planning frame from the previous lesson and either *The Sun* or *Night Fishing* as a model.

- Some children may prefer to work in pairs. Others could illustrate their poems or use a computer.

Plenary

- Share some poems and evaluate using a response sandwich, referring to the checklist.

- *Which similes were particularly successful? Why? Was alliteration used? Were powerful verbs used?*

Rhyme Banks

Objectives

We will compare and contrast poems about boys. We will also identify some of the features and styles used by poets, for example, the rhyme pattern, and we will learn to use a rhyming dictionary

You need: Resource Pages D–F and I; rhyming dictionaries; coloured pens, pencils or highlighters; whiteboards or notepads.

Whole class work

- Read and enjoy *My Brother Bert* (Resource Page D).

- In pairs, the children discuss which verse or verses they liked the best and why.

- The children highlight or underline rhyming pairs in different colours. Revise the fact that the rhyming words often use different phonemes, for example 'B<u>er</u>t' and 'sh<u>ir</u>t'.

- Read *Johnny's Pockets* (Resource Page E) and ask the children to compare and contrast it to the first poem. ***Which features do they have in common? Which features are unique to each poem? Which poem do they prefer and why?***

- Identify the rhyming words in *Johnny's Pockets* and explain that these make up the rhyming pattern of the poem, which can be annotated using letters (see Resource Page F).

- Add 'Poems may rhyme' to the structure checklist (see Resource Page I).

- ***What is similar about all the rhyming words in this poem?*** Answer: they are all nouns.

- Explain to your class that their task today will be to create a rhyme bank they can use to help them write a poem inspired by *Johnny's Pockets*.

Independent, pair or guided work

- Using whiteboards or notepads, the children brainstorm a list of items that they could keep in their pockets or bags.

- The children generate several words that rhyme with the items. (If they cannot think of at least one suitable rhyming word, then they need to discard the original item.)

- ***The more words you can find the better, because this will give you lots to choose from when you write your poem.***

- Photocopy the whiteboards.

Plenary

- ***Did anyone find any words for which you couldn't think of many rhymes?*** Challenge the children to think of a rhyme for 'orange'. (They won't!)

- Try to use standard English throughout. However, some children who have strong accents or who have English as an additional language may come up with rhymes that others would not recognise. These should be allowed.

- Explain that generating a rhyme bank can be very useful for writing poetry that rhymes and is a good planning method.

Using Alliteration

Objectives

We will compare and contrast poems about spiders, identify similes and alliteration, and use them in our own writing

You need: Resource Pages G–I; whiteboards; dictionaries.

Whole class work

- Explain that you are going to read two poems on the same subject but by different poets. Ask the children to try to visualise what is happening in each poem and to be ready to discuss them (compare and contrast) when you have finished. Read the two spider poems (Resource Pages G and H).

- Elicit their personal preference, with reasons, and analyse poems referring to the checklist (Resource Page I).

- Discuss *I Heard a Spider Sobbing* in general and then focus on the alliteration. **Is it successful? Why?**

- Brainstorm other nouns and verbs beginning with 's' that would fit into the style of the poem.

- Demonstrate how to use ideas from the brainstorm to make more lines for the poem. Ensure you model the use of all different senses, that is what you see, hear, feel, smell, touch in the web.

Independent, pair or guided work

- The children choose a letter and brainstorm words beginning with that letter. (You may wish to steer them away from 'difficult' letters such as 'x', 'y', 'z' or the poems will be very short!)

- The children create an alliterative spider poem that refers to all the different senses.

- Some children could illustrate their poems, or write them on the computer.

Plenary

- Ask the children to choose what they feel is their best line to read out to the class.

- Collect all the best lines to make a class display.

Two poems

Goldfish

Orange shapes
Dart to and fro,
Going up for food
Then diving down below.

Tails flap
Side by side,
Gills open
Bubbles rise.

Round and through
The weed they go,
Darting with sudden moves
Then still and slow.

Russell Howell

Night Fishing

If stars were minnows
they would flash across
the river of night, hiding
in its dark waters from
Fisherman-in-the-moon.

Moira Andrew

(Exemplar material)

Moon brainstorm

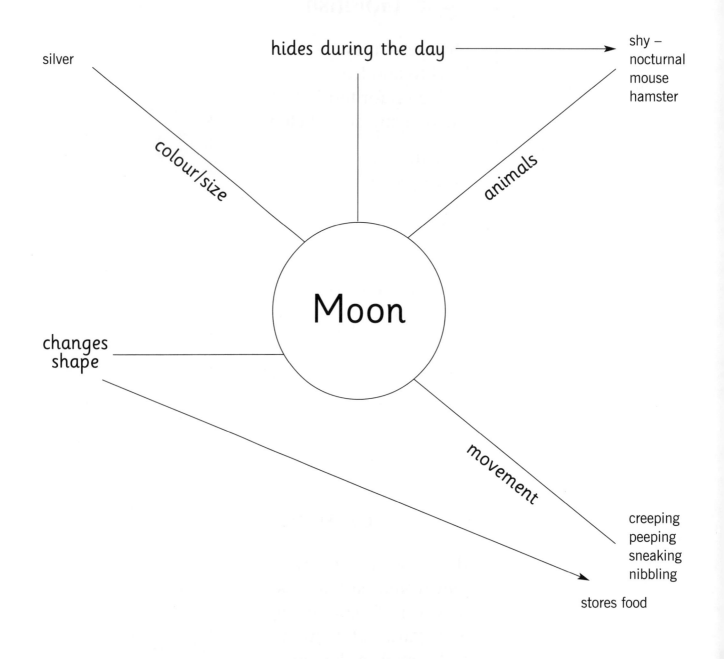

silver

hides during the day ──────────────→ shy –
nocturnal
mouse
hamster

colour/size

animals

Moon

changes
shape

movement

creeping
peeping
sneaking
nibbling

stores food

The Sun

The sun is a glowing spider
that crawls out
from under the earth
to make her way across the sky
warming and weaving
with her bright old fingers
of light.

Grace Nichols

(Pupil copymaster)

My Brother Bert

Pets are the hobby of my brother Bert.
He used to go to school with a Mouse in his shirt.

His hobby, it grew, as some hobbies will,
And it grew and GREW and GREW until

Oh, don't breathe a word, and pretend you haven't heard.
A simply appalling thing has occurred –

The very thought makes me iller and iller;
Bert's brought home a gigantic Gorilla!

If you think that's really not such a scare,
What if it quarrels with his Grizzly Bear?

You still think you could keep your head?
What if the Lion from under his bed

And the four Ostriches that deposit
Their football eggs in his bedroom closet

And the Aardvark out of his bottom drawer
All danced and joined in the roar?

What if the Pangolins were to caper
Out of their nests behind the wallpaper?

With the fifty sorts of Bats
That hang on his hat-stand like old hats,

And out of the shoebox the excitable Platypus
Along with the Ocelot or Jungle-Cattypus?

The Wombat, the Dingo, the Gecko, the Grumpus –
How they would shake the house with their rumpus!

Not to forget the Bandycoot
Who would certainly peer from his battered old boot,

Why, it would be a dreadful day,
And what, oh what would the neighbours say?

Ted Hughes

Johnny's Pockets

Johnny collects
Conkers on strings,
Sycamore seeds
With aeroplane wings,
Green acorn cups,
Seaweed and shells,
Treasures from crackers
Like whistles and bells.

Johnny collects
Buttons and rings,
Bits of a watch,
Cog wheels and springs,
Half-eaten sweets,
Nuts, nails and screws,
That's why his pockets
Bulge out of his trews.

Alison Winn

Example of analysis of *Johnny's Pockets*

Rhyme pattern:

Johnny collects — A
Conkers on <u>strings</u>, — B
Sycamore seeds — C
With aeroplane <u>wings</u>, — B
Green acorn cups, — D
Seaweed and shells, — E
Treasures from crackers — F
Like whistles and bells. — E

Johnny collects — A
Buttons and <u>rings</u>, — B
Bits of a watch, — C
Cog wheels and <u>springs</u>, — B
Half-eaten sweets, — D
Nuts, nails and screws, — E
That's why his pockets — F
Bulge out of his trews. — E

Alison Winn

(Pupil coymaster)

Big Billy

There's a spider in the bathroom
With legs as thick as rope.
It lives behind the cupboard
Where my mother keeps the soap.
My sister calls it Billy,
She says it creeps each night
Into children's bedrooms
(when they turn out the light).

I lay and hear him coming.
I hear his spider breath,
Huffing up the passage
With gasps as dark as death.
I hide beneath my duvet
… but the sides they won't tuck in …
And I know he'll find a pathway
And I know that Billy'll win!

I know he's going to get me.
I know he's going to come
And he's going to eat my sister
And he's going to get my Mum …
He's going to eat the family,
He's going to eat us all
'Cos Billy's really awful …
… and he's coming up the hall!!!

Peter Dixon

Classworks Literacy Year 4 © Sue Plechowicz, Nelson Thornes Ltd 2003

(Pupil copymaster)

I Heard a Spider Sobbing

I heard a spider sobbing
Deep in an autumn day.
She was sobbing in the bushes
Where spiders spin away.

Her legs were wet with spider tears,
Her eyes as full as seas.
There were blisters on her fingers
And blisters on her knees.

I held her in my warm cup hands,
I watched her wipe her tears
And whisper things and tell me things
Of spiders and their fears.

"I cannot weave a web," she said
"I don't know how it goes.
It gets in such a muddle,
It tangles in my toes.

"The silk – it gets all muddled
It hooks up on my knees,
Then catches in the bushes
And blows in all the breeze.

"I cannot get it right," she cried,
"It's such an awful mess.
A great big spider tangle,
A massive blackbird nest.
The other spiders giggle
They crawl across to laugh
And call me clumsy fingers
And say that I am daft.

"They always call me stupid,
They always make me cry
And I've never caught an insect,
    or moth
    or bug
    or fly.

"I've never caught a single thing,
My web's no good at all,
It's just a tatty tangle
A sort of cobweb ball.

"It's a great big mass of muddle
It's a matted messy mat.
It fell off all the bushes
And it landed on the cat."

I gazed upon the sleeping Tom
The tortured web hung dead.
A weave of tangled tangles ….
… the spider shook her head.

Her eyes again were flooded.
A sobbing shook my hand
So,
I took her very gently
To a special kind of land…
A land I know for spiders
Who cannot weave a trap
Where everyone is happy
With spiders big and fat.
A land of flies and honey
A land where all is lace,
And no-one needs to worry
    or spin
    or weave
    or race.

My land is very secret,
I cannot tell you where.
But if you ask a spider
then

    she

        might

           take you there.

Sue Plechowicz

Classworks Literacy Year 4 © Sue Plechowicz, Nelson Thornes Ltd 2003

(Exemplar material)

Checklist and model for poetry on a common theme

Example of a checklist for writing a poem ①

Structure

- Subject of poem needs to be researched
- Can use other poems as a frame for our own
- Poems may rhyme

Language features

- Use adjectives
- Use powerful verbs
- Use alliteration
- Use similes
- Use adverbs

Example of modelled writing from a plan ②

The Moon is a Mouse

If the moon were an animal,
it would be a shy mouse
sneaking out in the shadowy night
feeding on starlight,
until the sun lion,
king of the day
wakes up
and pounces.

(**Marking ladder**)

Name: _____

Pupil	Objective	Teacher
	I was inspired by the poem _____.	
	I have kept to a rhyme pattern using sensible rhymes.	
	My verbs are powerful.	
	My adjectives are strong.	
	I used alliteration.	
	I used similes.	
	What could I do to improve my poem next time?	

Instructions

Outcome

Ability to give and follow clear instructions; a mathematical game

Objectives

Sentence

1 to reread own writing to check for grammatical sense (coherence) and accuracy (agreement); to identify errors and to suggest alternative constructions.

Text

22 to identify features of instructional texts including: noting the intended outcome at the beginning; listing materials or ingredients; clearly set out sequential stages; language of commands, e.g. imperative verbs.

25 to write clear instructions using conventions learned from reading.

26 to improve the cohesion of written instructions and directions through the use of link phrases and organisational devices such as sub-headings and numbering.

Speaking and listening

• to give and follow a set of verbal instructions.

ICT

• to use cut and paste to reorder a piece of text.

Planning frame

• Give and follow verbal instructions focusing on clarity.

• Identify features of instructional texts.

• Write an instructional text.

• In conjunction with work in maths lessons, design and make a board game.

How you could plan this unit

Day 1	Day 2	Day 3	Day 3 (cont.)	Day 4
Speaking and listening	Reading and analysis	Writing Ask the children to follow a set of instructions that are not in a sensible order. Discuss different ways of ordering instructions: numbering/sequential connectives. Using ICT, sequence a set of instructions.	In maths lesson: plan a board game based on doubling (Resource Page C)	Writing
Verbal Instructions	*Recipes*			*Board Games* **In maths lesson:** Draw board for doubles game

Day 5
Writing Model turning the plan into instructions for a game. The children do the same, then use their marking ladder to evaluate (Resource Page E) **In maths lesson:** Try out game instructions and add to the board

81

Verbal Instructions

Objectives

We will discover that instructions need to be clear, and we will learn to give and follow a set of instructions

You need: click-together bricks (enough for each pair of children to have a duplicate set of 6 to 8 bricks of various sizes and colours); a video clip of a TV cookery programme in which the presenter repeats 'and then...', 'next you...' whilst demonstrating a recipe; instructional books.

Whole class work

- Introduce the genre of instructions: *Instructions tell you how to do or make something.* Explain that instructions can be written or verbal.

- Brainstorm common forms of instructional texts:
  - recipes
  - lists of rules
  - road signs
  - sewing and knitting patterns
  - washing instructions on labels/cooking instructions on packets
  - technical manuals, for example for cars, computers, TV
  - non-fiction books for example, 'How to draw', sports skills
  - board games.

- Give your teaching assistant (or a child) a set of click-together bricks and ask them to turn so they cannot see what you are doing. Build something with your own duplicate set of bricks. Say: *I want you to follow my instructions so that you make a building exactly the same as mine.* Give the instructions but do not make them clear. For example, if there are two different-sized blue bricks, don't clarify which one, or which direction a brick should be facing and so on. Then compare buildings.

- Ask the children: *What was wrong with my instructions?*

- Establish that verbal instructions need to be very clear and precise.

- Repeat the activity, this time being clear and allowing the person following the instructions to ask questions for clarification.

Independent, pair or guided work

- Arrange the room so the children can sit with their backs to each other. Ask them to take it in turns to give/follow instructions to build something.

- The children could also do this activity by giving each other instructions to draw something. It could also be used in maths, linked to work on 2D shape.

Plenary

- Ensure that they understand that both verbal and written instructions must be clear.

- Show the video clip, directing the children to listen to how the presenter lets you know that they've finished one thing and they are moving on to the next.

- Establish that in verbal instructions the words 'next' or 'then' are used constantly, but this would be boring if written and could even make instructions less clear.

- Look at some texts and collect alternative ways of signalling when to move on to the next instruction: sequential connectives, numbers, bullet points, sub-headings.

Recipes

Objective

We will identify the features of instructional texts

You need: Resource Pages A–D; instructional books.

Whole class work

- Display the recipe (Resource Page A). Read through and brainstorm the structural and language features (see Resource Pages B and D for ideas). Discuss each one and record on a class checklist.

  - *Why do we need a goal at the beginning?* It tells the reader what is going to be the end result.

  - *Why is it useful to have a list of equipment at the beginning?* So the reader has it ready and would not be distracted by having to get equipment during the process.

  - *What techniques could be used to indicate that the instructions need to be read in order?* Numbers, sequential connectives, arrows.

  - *Why are diagrams and illustrations useful?* To give the reader a visual reference for the end result or stages leading to the end result.

  - *What kind of additional information could be put in a separate box?* Technical language that may be unfamiliar to readers.

  - *Where are the verbs?* Usually at the beginning of the sentence because instructions are written like orders – in the imperative.

  - *What tense?* The present, because it is as if the writer is giving verbal instructions for the reader to follow as they go along.

  - *What person is it written in?* Second, because all references to people are general rather than specific.

  - *What kind of language is used?* In order to keep instructions clear, only necessary details are included. Simple, precise sentences using adjectives and adverbs for clarity and precision not for effect (as they would be in fiction writing).

Independent, pair or guided work

- Using a range of instructional texts photocopied from books in the school library, the children identify and highlight examples of the features on the checklist.

Plenary

- *Did you find most or all the features on the checklist in your text?*

- Introduce the planning frame (see Resource Page C for layout). Ask the children to think about how it could be used to organise the basic planning of an instructional text. (Answer: The instructions could be written inside the circles to ensure they are sequenced properly. What you need at each stage could be written alongside the relevant circle and then later collated.)

- Explain that you will be using the frame to help you plan a set of instructions.

Board Games

Objectives

We will write clear instructions for a board game planned in a maths lesson, then reread our work to check for clarity and accuracy

You need: Resource Page C; whiteboards.

Whole class work

- Remind the children of the features of an instructional text by going through the class checklist from the previous lesson.

- Focus on verbs. Remind the children that they are in the imperative present tense.

- Give some instructions such as:

> Go and open the door, please.
> Get me a pencil, please.

- Ask the children to write a short instruction for their partner on their whiteboard, ensuring that they use imperative present tense (verb first) but also that they are polite!

- *Check if your partner has put the verb first. Is it in the present tense?*

- Now ask the children to add an adverb. First discuss where it should go in the sentence to ensure it makes sense, still keeping the verb first.

- The children share their instruction with their partner and if they both agree that it makes sense, their partner should follow the instruction.

- Using Resource Page C, model putting the maths game on to the planning frame so that you can be sure that it makes sense before you actually make the game. Refer to the checklist and 'think aloud':

> Write the 'outcome' in the goal box.
>
> Write the step by step instructions in the circles (verb first) and number them so players are sure of the order they need to do things in, or perhaps use connectives like 'Next you …'
>
> Write the 'You need…' section.
>
> Write a final comment at the end, such as 'Enjoy playing!'
>
> Include a diagram of the equipment and a box to explain that doubling is multiplying by two.

Independent, pair or guided work

- The children write their own 'doubling' game on to a blank planning frame. Some children may want to use the same layout, but some may wish to change the colours, the score or add different penalties, for example: 'Start again from zero' or 'Go back two places'.

Plenary

- In pairs, the children talk through their plan to see if the instructions are clear and if the game will work.

Pupil copymaster

A tasty recipe

Follow this recipe carefully and you will make delicious cheese on toast.

You need …
100g cheddar cheese, grated
2 thick slices of bread
butter

Steps

1. Switch on the oven grill.

2. Place the bread on the grill pan and put it under the grill.

3. When the bread is golden brown, take it out from under the grill.

4. Spread a thin layer of butter on the untoasted sides of the bread. *Do not use too much butter or the bread will go soggy.*

5. Sprinkle the grated cheese onto the buttered sides of the toast.

6. Then put the bread and cheese back under the grill.

7. When the cheese melts and turns a golden brown, carefully remove from under the grill.

Eat and enjoy!

Note: *Any hard, tasty cheese can be used for this recipe. Why not try Red Leicester next time?*

Classworks Literacy Year 4 © Sue Plechowicz, Nelson Thornes Ltd 2003

(Exemplar analysis)

Example of analysis of *A tasty recipe*

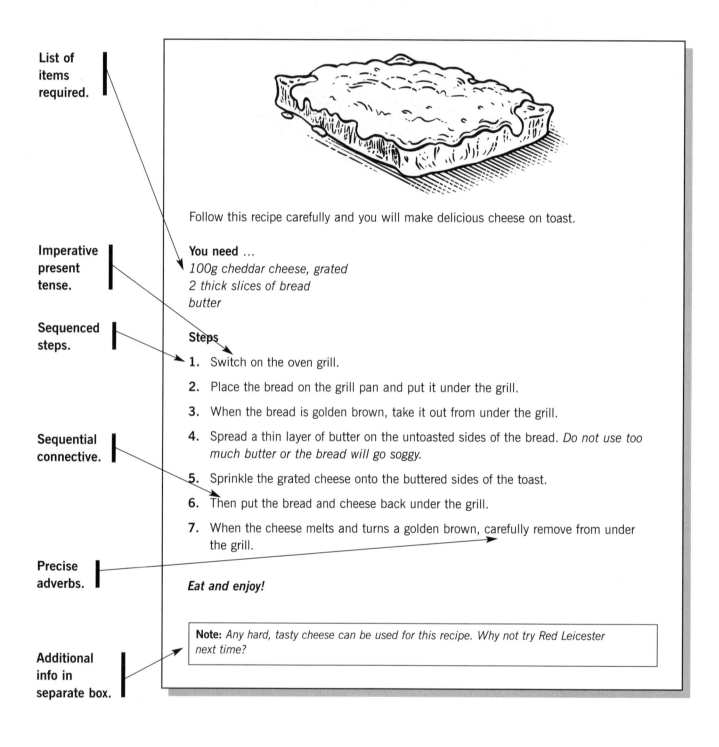

List of items required.

Imperative present tense.

Sequenced steps.

Sequential connective.

Precise adverbs.

Additional info in separate box.

Follow this recipe carefully and you will make delicious cheese on toast.

You need …
100g cheddar cheese, grated
2 thick slices of bread
butter

Steps

1. Switch on the oven grill.

2. Place the bread on the grill pan and put it under the grill.

3. When the bread is golden brown, take it out from under the grill.

4. Spread a thin layer of butter on the untoasted sides of the bread. *Do not use too much butter or the bread will go soggy.*

5. Sprinkle the grated cheese onto the buttered sides of the toast.

6. Then put the bread and cheese back under the grill.

7. When the cheese melts and turns a golden brown, carefully remove from under the grill.

Eat and enjoy!

Note: *Any hard, tasty cheese can be used for this recipe. Why not try Red Leicester next time?*

Pupil copymaster

Plan of game

Play this game to practise adding, rounding and doubling numbers.

You need ...
2 counters
Pen
Paper
2 dice

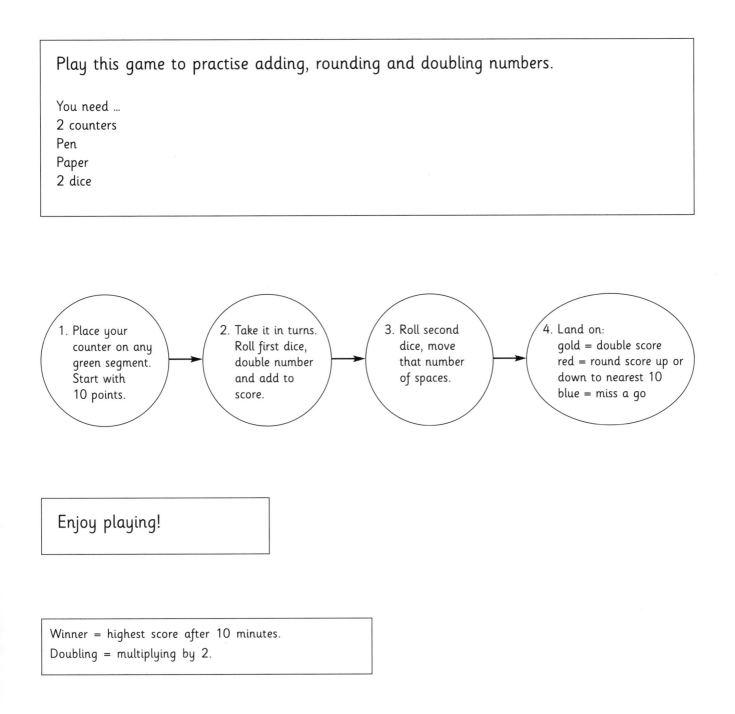

1. Place your counter on any green segment. Start with 10 points.

2. Take it in turns. Roll first dice, double number and add to score.

3. Roll second dice, move that number of spaces.

4. Land on:
gold = double score
red = round score up or down to nearest 10
blue = miss a go

Enjoy playing!

Winner = highest score after 10 minutes.
Doubling = multiplying by 2.

(Exemplar material)

Checklist for instructions

Structure

- Start by stating the goal

- List items needed

- Instructions should be in sequenced steps

- May have additional information in a separate box

- Diagrams are often included

Language features

- Imperative present tense (verb first)

- Sequential (time) connectives

- Clear, precise language

- Adverbs chosen for clarity not vividness

- Written in second person ('you')

Marking ladder

Name: _____

Pupil	Objective	Teacher
	I started by stating the goal.	
	I listed the items needed.	
	I wrote instructions in sequenced steps.	
	I used numbers, bullet points or time connectives.	
	I added additional information in a separate box.	
	I used diagrams to make it clearer.	
	I put the verbs first and in the present tense.	
	My instructions are written in the second person.	
	I used clear, precise language.	
	What could I do to improve my instructions next time?	

Playscripts

Outcome

Playscript developed and extended by the class for performance

Objectives

Sentence

3 to identify the use of powerful verbs, e.g. 'hobbled' instead of 'went'.

4 to identify adverbs and understand their functions in sentences through: identifying common adverbs with '-ly' suffix and discussing their impact on the meaning of sentences; using adverbs with greater discrimination in own writing.

Text

5 to prepare, read and perform playscripts; compare organisation of scripts with stories – how are settings indicated, story lines made clear?

6 to chart the build-up of a play scene, e.g. how scenes start, how dialogue is expressed, and how scenes are concluded.

13 to write playscripts, e.g. using known stories as basis.

Speaking and listening

● Drama Activities – improvisation and role play: interpret a range of stimulus material; recognise how the roles in situations can be approached from different viewpoints.

Planning frame

● Read and analyse features of playscripts.

● Chart the build-up of a play scene.

● Improve a script by adding extra parts and stage directions.

● Write an additional scene.

● Improvise and role-play characters.

● Perform/direct a play.

Note

● This unit can be linked to R.E.

How you could plan this unit

Day 1	Day 2	Day 3	Day 4	Day 5
Reading and analysis	Reading and writing	Writing and analysis Identify how the lines in the poem *The Queen of Hearts* are built into a script (Resource Page C). Discuss the notion that God created humans to care for animals/the environment. The children write dialogue (see Resource Page D)	Reading and writing	Analysis and drama Using Resource Page C, demonstrate that writers and actors consider how characters would behave. Role play or hot seat activities
Main Features	*The Narrator*		*Stage Directions*	

Day 6	Day 7	Day 8	Day 9	Day 10
Writing	Writing and analysis Demonstrate how to refer to checklists to make a marking ladder for writing playscripts. Model marking own script (Resource Pages I and J)	Writing Prepare a class script to add to *The Busy Day*, using the best examples from Day 6. Demonstrate how to improve writing. The children continue to check class play	Drama In small groups, the children act/direct *The Busy Day* including the scene written by your class. Allow time for each group to perform to the others. Did actors use stage directions?	Performance Each group performs to a different audience. Some work on costumes, stage design, photos, videoing, introduction, invitations and so on (this activity can extend into following days)
Script-writing				

Main Features

Objective

We will investigate the features of playscripts

You need: Resource Pages A, B, D and I.

Whole class work

- Display *A Jumble for the Queen* (Resource Pages A and B). **How do you know this is a play?** Highlight any features (such as cast list, characters' names on left, scenes rather than chapters) that the children identify. Start to compile a class checklist (see Resource Page I for ideas).

- Choose six children to read the parts of the characters. Discuss the fact that the speech comes after the character's name and that it does not have speech marks around it.

- Before they start, explain that the play is a historical one set in Elizabethan times. Brainstorm what they know about Elizabethan times.

  A 'jumble' was a type of biscuit.

- When the readers have finished, ask them what helped them to add expression to the words. Establish that the punctuation is useful (! and ?).

- **Can you identify any more features to put on the checklist?**

Independent, pair or guided work

- In pairs, the children read *The Busy Day* (Resource Page D). The children identify and highlight the features that indicate it is a playscript.

Plenary

- Share findings.

- **What were your initial thoughts about this play? What did you like/dislike? Why?**

The Narrator

Objective

We will understand the role of the narrator in a playscript

You need: Resource Pages C and E.

Whole class work

- Read your class the poem *The Queen of Hearts* if they are not familiar with it:

> The Queen of Hearts
> She made some tarts,
> All on a summer's day.
> The Knave of Hearts
> He stole the tarts,
> And took them clean away.
>
> The King of Hearts
> Called for the tarts,
> And beat the Knave full score.
> The Knave of Hearts
> Brought back the tarts,
> And vowed he'd steal no more.

- Display *The Queen of Hearts* script (Resource Page C).

- Choose five children to read the parts of the characters. Read through.

- Ask the children to discuss with their response partners the role of the narrator. Share ideas:

> The narrator sets the scene.
>
> The narrator explains what is happening.
>
> The narrator gives background information.

- Identify what particular role the narrator is playing in each of the speeches in the play.

Independent, pair or guided work

- In pairs, the children write a part for a narrator in the excerpt from *The Busy Day* (Resource Page E).

Plenary

- Choose some children to share their work.

- Add the role of narrator to the class checklist.

Note

- For subsequent lessons on *The Busy Day* you will need a version of the script that includes a part for the narrator. This can possibly be prepared by your more able group.

Stage Directions

Objective

We will discuss the need for stage directions in playscripts, and discover why they should use powerful verbs and adverbs

You need: Resource Pages D (amended version including narrator), F and G; whiteboards.

Whole class work

- Display *Charlie and the Chocolate Factory* script (Resource Page F).

- Choose five children to read the parts of the characters. Refer to the fact that there is no cast list – this is unhelpful.

- Remind the children that they should not read the words in brackets.

- ***What is the purpose of the words in brackets?*** Answer: they tell the actors what to do and help the director (or reader) to build up a vivid picture. Explain that these are called stage directions.

- ***What kind of words are used in the stage directions?*** Answer: powerful verbs and adverbs.

- The children list four powerful verbs and two adverbs from the text stage directions on their whiteboards.

> grabs, pops, wringing, shaking, backing
>
> sadly, helplessly

- Discuss how the action would change if you replaced some of the verbs and adverbs with different ones. Try replacing *[Sighing and shaking head sadly]* with *[Stamping foot and shaking head angrily]*.

- Using the amended class copy of *The Busy Day* (Resource Page D), model how to add some stage directions to the first couple of speeches (Resource Page G).

Independent, pair or guided work

- In groups of six, read through the play one speech at a time. The children discuss and agree upon the stage directions that are needed. Add to individual scripts.

Plenary

- Each group tells the rest of the class one stage direction that they have added to a particular speech.

- Add these to the class copy.

- Remind the children that the punctuation is also a kind of stage direction, particularly exclamation marks, pauses and question marks.

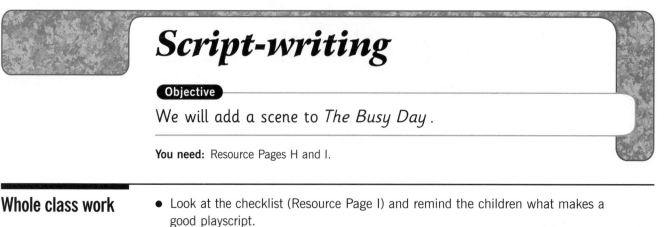

Script-writing

Objective

We will add a scene to *The Busy Day*.

You need: Resource Pages H and I.

Whole class work

- Look at the checklist (Resource Page I) and remind the children what makes a good playscript.

- Explain that they are going to write a new scene for *The Busy Day* in which the angels are going to be discussing what it was like during the week of creation.

- Discuss what happened on each day (see right). It will be helpful if this has previously been discussed in R.E.

> THE CHRISTIAN/JEWISH STORY OF CREATION
>
> Day 1 – Light
>
> Day 2 – Heaven and Earth
>
> Day 3 – Seas, land and trees
>
> Day 4 – Sun, moon and stars
>
> Day 5 – Birds and fish
>
> Day 6 – Animals and humans
>
> Day 7 – God rested

- Model writing the narrator setting the scene and the Archangel talking about the first day of creation (Resource Page H). Ensure that you refer to the class checklist (see Resource Page I) as you 'talk aloud' the process.

Independent, pair or guided work

- The children write a script for one of the remaining days of creation – make sure all the days are covered. You could give them the following framework to start with:

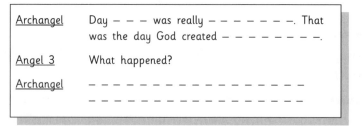

> Archangel   Day – – – was really – – – – – – –. That
>   was the day God created – – – – – – – –.
>
> Angel 3   What happened?
>
> Archangel   –
>   – – – – – – – – – – – – – – – – – – –

Plenary

- Share an example for each day.

- ***How did the character (God) develop across the week? What sort of different 'Gods' were there?*** (happy, tired, excited?)

- Use a response sandwich to evaluate: one good comment, one idea for improvement, another good comment.

(Pupil copymaster)

A Jumble for the Queen

Cast: *Narrator*
Percival Platter – pastry cook to Sir Richard Ash
Joan – kitchenhand
Tom – Joan's schoolboy brother, aged 10
Tom's schoolmaster
Queen Elizabeth I
London crowd

Scene 1

Narrator It's seven of the clock and a fine summer morning.

Percival Too fine! I'm sweating already. And I can't find the minced dates.

Narrator In Sir Richard Ash's house in Kent everyone is busy: the serving man and the stable lads, the butlers and the brewers, the carvers and the chambermaids …

Percival And the cooks!

Narrator How many cooks?

Percival I'm too busy to count. But not enough pastry cooks. Joan! Joan! Where is that little lie-a-bed?

Joan I'm not lying in bed! I'm here and I'm cutting herbs.

Percival Cutting herbs! What about the custard tarts? Don't you know the Queen comes here tonight?

Joan Yes, Mr Platter. How could I not know? But the mistress said she needed some more herbs to strew on the floor. She said the Queen likes the smell of them.

Percival The Queen likes the taste of custard tarts, that's all I care about, and she won't be getting any at this rate. Now, run along to the dairy and fetch some more milk.

Joan Yes, sir.

Percival Where did I put those minced dates? We'll never be ready in time!

Scene 2

Narrator Seven-fifteen of the clock, and Joan's brother Tom is late for school.

Master And where is your cap, Thomas?

Tom It … it blew away, sir!

Master I could beat you for being late, Thomas, and I could beat you for losing your cap. Do you want to be beaten?

Tom No, Sir.

Master What is that on your satchel, Thomas?

Tom Nothing, Sir.

Master Yes it is, it's your cap, and it's wet. Why is it wet, Thomas?

Tom I … I was catching frogs in it on the way to school, Sir.

Master I think perhaps you do want to be beaten after all, Thomas.

Scene 3

Narrator Ten of the clock, and the Queen is leaving London. Not just the Queen. Hundreds of people and thousands of horses. Wagons full of clothes and jewels, pictures, books, bed-clothes …

Queen And beer. Weak beer. Of all things, I detest strong beer.

Narrator The people of London throng the streets to watch the magnificent procession pass by.

Everyone Long live the Queen!

Queen I thank you, good people of London. I am leaving you now for the fair county of Kent. But though I am away, may your love for me remain in your hearts till I return.

Everyone God bless the Queen!

Classworks Literacy Year 4 © Sue Plechowicz, Nelson Thornes Ltd 2003

A Jumble for the Queen (continued)

<table>
<tr><td colspan="2">

Scene 4

</td><td colspan="2">

Scene 5

</td></tr>
<tr>
<td>Narrator</td>
<td>Half-past ten of the clock. In Sir Richard's kitchen the custard tarts are all made.</td>
<td>Narrator</td>
<td>Eleven of the clock, and the schoolboys are having their dinner.</td>
</tr>
<tr>
<td>Percival</td>
<td>But not the quince pies! Joan! Joan! What are you doing with the vinegar? You should be peeling quinces.</td>
<td>Master</td>
<td>Thomas, don't cut your nails at the table!</td>
</tr>
<tr>
<td>Joan</td>
<td>But the mistress asked me to make some tooth soap first.</td>
<td>Tom</td>
<td>I'm sorry, sir.</td>
</tr>
<tr>
<td>Percival</td>
<td>Tooth soap! Tooth soap! What do we want with tooth soap at a time like this?</td>
<td>Master</td>
<td>What is the proper use of a penknife, Thomas?</td>
</tr>
<tr>
<td>Joan</td>
<td>The mistress thought the Queen might need some for her teeth after eating all our puddings.</td>
<td>Tom</td>
<td>For shaping quills into pens, sir.</td>
</tr>
<tr>
<td>Percival</td>
<td>She can't eat the puddings if we haven't finished making them!</td>
<td>Master</td>
<td>And how do you say in Latin, 'The boy who cuts his nails with a penknife will be beaten'?</td>
</tr>
<tr>
<td>Joan</td>
<td>It won't be long, sir. I've mixed the vinegar and white wine. I just need to add the honey and then boil it up.</td>
<td>Tom</td>
<td>Er … 'puer', that's 'the boy'. 'Puer …' I don't know the rest, sir.</td>
</tr>
<tr>
<td>Percival</td>
<td>But what about the quince pies? We'll never be ready in time!</td>
<td>Master</td>
<td>And you didn't know your Latin poem this morning. Latin is the key to all knowledge, Thomas, haven't I told you that?</td>
</tr>
<tr>
<td></td>
<td></td>
<td>Tom</td>
<td>Yes, you have, sir.</td>
</tr>
<tr>
<td></td>
<td></td>
<td>Master</td>
<td>I have told you in words, Thomas, but now I think that perhaps the birch rod will speak to you better than I can. You will bring me the rod after dinner, Thomas.</td>
</tr>
<tr>
<td></td>
<td></td>
<td>Tom</td>
<td>Oh no, sir, please, sir, no!</td>
</tr>
<tr>
<td></td>
<td></td>
<td>Master</td>
<td>Oh yes, Thomas!</td>
</tr>
</table>

Julia Donaldson, Story & Drama Toolkit *(The Bible Society)*

(**Pupil copymaster**)

The Queen of Hearts – a play

Cast: *Queen of Hearts*
King of Hearts
Prime Minister
Knave of Hearts (son of King and Queen)
Narrator

Narrator	The scene is the kitchen of Heart Castle.
Queen	It's a lovely day. Just the sort of day to do some baking. I think I'll make some jam tarts.
Narrator	The Queen makes some tarts and leaves them to cool.
Knave	What's that lovely smell? Mmm! It's coming from the kitchen window. I bet Mum's made some of her delicious tarts.
Narrator	The Knave follows his nose to the open kitchen window.
Knave	Oooh! Yum! I love Mum's jam tarts. I'm sure nobody would notice if I had just one … Mmm! I think I'll have another …
Narrator	The tarts are so delicious that the Knave takes the rest and disappears to his room. Just then the smell of baking reaches the King.
King	Queenie dear! Shall we have some of those tarts for tea?
Queen	Good idea, I'll just get some … Aaah! My tarts! Where are they? I put them here to cool. Someone's stolen my tarts!
Narrator	The King sends for his Prime Minister.
King	I want you to investigate a theft. The Queen's jam tarts have been stolen.
Prime Minister	I know just how to solve this problem, Your Majesty. Send for all the people in the palace.
Narrator	The people line up in front of the King and the Prime Minister. The Prime Minister walks slowly down the line. He stops in front of the Knave.
Prime Minister	Here's the culprit, Your Majesty.
King	How do you know?
Prime Minister	Easy! Look around his mouth. What do you see?
King	Oh! Jam!
Knave	I didn't mean it, I didn't mean to, I was so hungry.
Narrator	The King punishes the Knave for stealing the tarts.
King	Where are the rest of the tarts?
Knave	I'll go and get them straight away.
Narrator	The Knave rushes off then returns with the tarts. He gives them to the King.
Knave	I'm so sorry, Dad. I promise I'll never steal again.

Classworks Literacy Year 4 © Sue Plechowicz, Nelson Thornes Ltd 2003

(Pupil copymaster)

The Busy Day

Cast: Archangel
Four junior angels

Scene 1 – Heaven

Archangel	What a day! What a day! These have been the six busiest days of my life! I've not had a moment's rest since God started creating. What's more, He now wants detailed records of all the animals. Being a member of the heavenly host is not what it used to be. Personally I used to enjoy a bit of harp playing with my feet up on a cloud, but there's no time for that these days. No time at all! Where are those junior angels? God promised me some help but they are never around when you need them … Ah, there you are!
Angel 1	Sorry we're late.
Angel 2	Sorry.
Angel 3	Sorry.
Angel 4	Sorry.
Archangel	Right now, there's a lot of work to be done. You, Angel 1, I want you to read out a description of each animal. Angel 2, you should check to see if it is correct. Angel 3, I want you to read out its purpose, and Angel 4, I want you to stamp and file the finished record. Is that clear?
Angels	Yes, Archangel.
Archangel	Right, let's begin. Animal 223459870: SHEEP.
Angel 1	White woolly thing, four legs, eats grass.
Angel 2	Correct.
Angel 3	Gives us woolly jumpers and cuts down on lawnmowers.
Angel 4	Filed!
Archangel	Animal 33307779: SPIDER.
Angel 1	Six legs, sometimes hairy, catches flies.
Angel 2	Incorrect. It has eight legs.
Angel 3	Frightens some humans, cuts down on fly spray.
Angel 4	Filed!
Archangel	Animal 44670001: HUMAN BEING.
Angel 1	Large brain, noisy, comes in a variety of shapes and sizes.
Angel 2	Correct.
Angel 3	[silence]
Archangel	What's the matter, Angel 3? Is there a problem?
Angel 3	I don't know what humans are for. They don't eat grass or flies so God couldn't have made them to keep the grass short or reduce the fly population. I just don't know what they're for.
Archangel	Does anyone else know?
Angels	No.
Archangel	God must have had some reason for making them. After all, He has made rather a lot of them. I happen to know he took a great deal of trouble over their design.
Angel 1	Maybe God made them to tidy up the place. The trees are terribly untidy, especially in Autumn.
Angel 2	I think they're just for decoration. Some of them are quite good looking.
Angel 3	Perhaps they're meant to keep the animals under control. Some animals are very badly behaved, especially the monkeys.
Angel 4	Maybe God made them to be His friends. He might just enjoy their company.
All	You must be joking!
Archangel	It's no good. I'll have to go back and ask God. Meet me back here tomorrow at six o'clock. Don't be late!

Margaret Cooling

Classworks Literacy Year 4 © Sue Plechowicz, Nelson Thornes Ltd 2003

(**Pupil copymaster**)

The Busy Day writing frame

Read through these extracts from *The Busy Day* and add speeches for the narrator that set the scene or explain what is happening.

Extract 1

Cast: *Archangel*
Four junior angels
Narrator

<u>Scene 1 – Heaven</u>

Narrator

Archangel   What a day! What a day! These have been the six busiest days of my life! I've not had a moment's rest since God started creating. What's more, He now wants detailed records of all the animals. Being a member of the heavenly host is not what it used to be. Personally I used to enjoy a bit of harp playing with my feet up on a cloud, but there's no time for that these days. No time at all! Where are those junior angels? God promised me some help but they are never around when you need them …

Narrator

Archangel   Ah, there you are!
Angel 1   Sorry we're late.
Angel 2   Sorry.
Angel 3   Sorry.
Angel 4   Sorry.

Extract 2

Angel 3   I don't know what humans are for. They don't eat grass or flies so God couldn't have made them to keep the grass short or reduce the fly population. I just don't know what they're for.
Archangel   Does anyone else know?
Angels   No.
Narrator

Charlie and the Chocolate Factory

VIOLET BEAUREGARDE	Just so long as it's gum, and I can chew it ... then that's for me! *[She takes her own piece of gum out of her mouth and sticks it behind her left ear]* Come on, Mr Wonka, hand over this magic gum of yours ... and we'll see if the thing works!
MRS BEAUREGARDE	Now, Violet ... let's not do anything silly.
VIOLET BEAUREGARDE	I want the gum! What's so silly?
WILLY WONKA	I would rather you didn't take it. You see, I haven't got it quite right yet. There are still one or two things ...
VIOLET BEAUREGARDE	*[Interrupting]* Oh, to heck with that *[She grabs the gum and pops it into her mouth]*
WILLY WONKA	Don't!
VIOLET BEAUREGARDE	Fabulous! It's great!
WILLY WONKA	Spit it out!
MR BEAUREGARDE	Keep chewing, kiddo! Keep right on chewing, baby! This is a great day for the Beauregardes! Our little girl is the first person in the world to have a chewing-gum meal!
WILLY WONKA	*[Wringing his hands]* No – no – no – no – no! It isn't for eating! You mustn't do it.
MRS BEAUREGARDE	Good heavens, girl! What's happening to your nose? It's turning blue!
VIOLET BEAUREGARDE	Oh, be quiet, mother, and let me finish!
MRS BEAUREGARDE	Your cheeks! Your chin! Your whole face is turning blue! Mercy save us! The girl's going blue and purple all over! Violet, you're turning violet, Violet! What is happening to you? You're glowing all over! The whole room is glowing!
WILLY WONKA	*[Sighing and shaking head sadly]* I told you I hadn't got it right. It always goes wrong when we come to the dessert. It's the blueberry pie that does it. But I'll get it right one day, you wait and see!
MRS BEAUREGARDE	Violet ... you're swelling up!
[VIOLET begins backing off stage]	
VIOLET BEAUREGARDE	I feel most peculiar!
MRS BEAUREGARDE	You're swelling up! You're blowing up like a balloon!
WILLY WONKA	Like a blueberry!
MRS BEAUREGARDE	Call a doctor!
MR SALT	Prick her with a pin!
MRS BEAUREGARDE	*[Wringing her hands helplessly]* Save her!
WILLY WONKA	It always happens like this. All the Oompa-Loompas that tried it finished up as blueberries. It's most annoying. I just can't understand it.

Adapted by Richard George from the book by Roald Dahl, in Moonlight, Seas and Chocolate Trees

(**Pupil copymaster**)

Modelling stage directions for *The Busy Day*

Archangel   *[Archangel bursts into the room looking flustered]* What a day! What a day! These have been the six busiest days of my life! I've not had a moment's rest since God started creating. What's more, He now wants detailed records of all the animals. Being a member of the heavenly host is not what it used to be. Personally I used to enjoy a bit of harp playing with my feet up on a cloud, but there's no time for that these days. No time at all! *[Looking all around and frowning]* Where are those junior angels? God promised me some help but they are never around when you need them …

[Enter four Angels with clipboards and pencils]

Archangel   *[Annoyed]* Ah, there you are!

Angel 1   *[Looking concerned]* Sorry we're late.

Angel 2   *[Sheepishly]* Sorry.

[The angels form a line]

Angel 3   Sorry.

Angel 4   Sorry.

(Exemplar analysis)

Example of analysis of *The Busy Day* – Scene 2

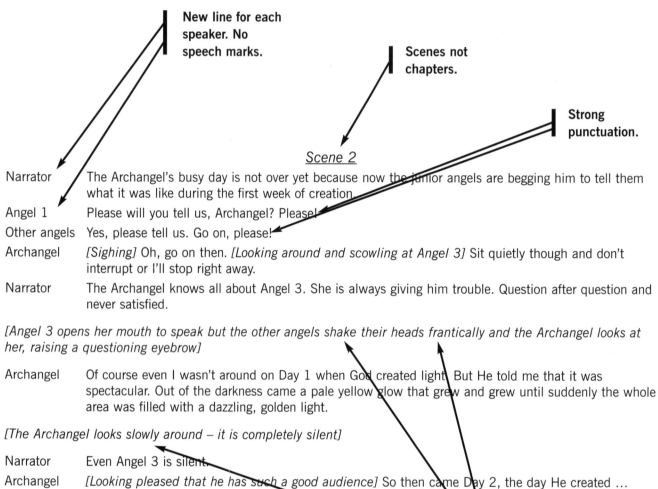

New line for each speaker. No speech marks.

Scenes not chapters.

Strong punctuation.

Scene 2

Narrator   The Archangel's busy day is not over yet because now the junior angels are begging him to tell them what it was like during the first week of creation.

Angel 1   Please will you tell us, Archangel? Please!

Other angels   Yes, please tell us. Go on, please!

Archangel   *[Sighing]* Oh, go on then. *[Looking around and scowling at Angel 3]* Sit quietly though and don't interrupt or I'll stop right away.

Narrator   The Archangel knows all about Angel 3. She is always giving him trouble. Question after question and never satisfied.

[Angel 3 opens her mouth to speak but the other angels shake their heads frantically and the Archangel looks at her, raising a questioning eyebrow]

Archangel   Of course even I wasn't around on Day 1 when God created light. But He told me that it was spectacular. Out of the darkness came a pale yellow glow that grew and grew until suddenly the whole area was filled with a dazzling, golden light.

[The Archangel looks slowly around – it is completely silent]

Narrator   Even Angel 3 is silent.

Archangel   *[Looking pleased that he has such a good audience]* So then came Day 2, the day He created ...

Stage directions. Include adverbs and powerful verbs.

(Exemplar material)

Checklist for playscripts

Structure

- Include a cast list at the start
- Narrator:
  - gives background info
  - sets scene
  - explains what is happening
- Step by step events take place in setting:
  - speakers' names on left
  - no speech marks
  - new line for each new speech
- Plays have scenes instead of chapters
- Put stage directions in brackets
- Use strong punctuation

Language features

- Stage directions use:
  - adverbs
  - powerful verbs

Classworks Literacy Year 4 © Sue Plechowicz, Nelson Thornes Ltd 2003

(**Marking ladder**)

Name: _____

Pupil	Objective	Teacher
	My script includes a cast list at the start.	
	It has a narrator.	
	The speakers' names are on the left.	
	I have not used speech marks.	
	I started a new line for each new speech.	
	My playscript has scenes.	
	I wrote stage directions in brackets.	
	I used adverbs and powerful verbs.	
	What could I do to improve my playscript next time?	

Stories That Raise Issues

Outcome

A short story about a dilemma; writing about how an issue may affect a character

Objectives

Sentence

1 to reread own writing to check for grammatical sense (coherence) and accuracy (agreement); to identify errors and to suggest alternative constructions.

Text

1 to identify social, moral or cultural issues in stories, e.g. the dilemmas faced by characters or the moral of the story, and to discuss how the characters deal with them; to locate evidence in text.

3 to understand how paragraphs or chapters are used to collect, order and build up ideas.

8 to write critically about an issue or dilemma raised in a story, explaining the problem, alternative courses of action and evaluating the writer's solution.

9 to read further stories or poems by a favourite writer, making comparisons and identifying familiar features of the writer's work.

11 to explore the main issues of a story by writing a story about a dilemma and the issues it raises for the character.

Speaking and listening

- to use hot seating; to accept response and feedback from others.

Planning frame

- Discuss issues and dilemmas and identify features in stories that raise issues of cheating and bullying.

- Write critically about the issue of bullying and alternative ways a character could deal with it.

- Explore how writers convey the feelings of their characters.

- Plan and write a story about a dilemma that raises issues for the characters.

Note

- You will need a copy of *Cheat*, by Judy Waite, in Heinemann Literacy World Essential Texts, or similar.

How you could plan this unit

Day 1	Day 2	Day 3	Day 4	Day 5
Reading and analysis	**Reading and writing** Discuss bullying, dilemmas and text features. Start a checklist (see Resource Page F). Read Resource Page A again and write critically about character's dilemma, explaining problem and possible action	**Writing** Model story hill for a story that raises an issue without giving away dilemma or resolution. The children write own plans	**Hot-seating and writing**	**Writing**
Issues and Dilemmas			*Hot-seating Characters*	*Writing the Introduction*

Day 6	Day 7	Day 8	Day 9	Day 10
Re-drafting Reread model introduction focusing on tense, person and rhetorical questions. The children improve own introductions then write out final copy	**Character planning** Model how to plan two main characters. The children plan own main characters	**Writing characters into story**	**Writing – story build-up**	**Re-drafting** Reread model build-up focusing on powerful verbs and using checklists. The children improve own build-up and then add to final copy
		Introducing Characters	*Using Flashbacks*	

Day 11	Day 12	Day 13	Day 14	Day 15
Writing dilemma Model writing dilemma showing use of 'maybe' and 'perhaps'. The children write their own dilemma section	**Writing** Reread model dilemma and use checklists. Focus on varying sentence length. The children improve own dilemma using long and short sentences. Add to final copy	**Writing resolution and ending** Model writing resolution – where dilemma is resolved. Compare to ending (reflective), and link back to introduction – may contain a cliffhanger	**Writing and evaluating** Model checking resolution and ending. Reread story. The children evaluate your story with marking ladder (Resource Page G). The children check own resolution and ending, add it to final copy, then evaluate	**Sharing stories** Read to other classes. The children could record their stories to ask other classes for feedback, or email them to other schools or to the authors who inspired them

Issues and Dilemmas

Objectives

We will identify issues in stories and discuss how characters deal with them. We will explore how writers deal with story dilemmas

You need: Resource Page A; a copy of *Cheat*, by Judy Waite, in Heinemann Literacy World Essential Texts or similar.

Whole class work

- Introduce the genre – stories with a dilemma that raises issues for the characters.

- *What is a dilemma?* Discuss answers and come up with a definition: **A dilemma is a situation in which a character has to make a difficult choice or decision.**

- Brainstorm some examples of dilemmas:

> What do you do if you know someone is being bullied?
>
> What if you get the chance to pass a test by cheating?
>
> Do you laugh or tease someone for being different because your friends do?

- Explain that dilemmas are often related to subjects such as cheating, bullying, stealing, racism, human rights, the environment, jealousy. These are called 'issues'. – subjects about which people often disagree and which require you to make choices about how to behave.

- Read *Cheat*, by Judy Waite (or similar story). Ask the children to think about the issue and the dilemmas Danny was faced with.

    - *What is the issue?* Cheating. *How has Danny cheated?* Saying the painting was his. Pretending he is better than he is.

    - *Why do you think Danny felt worse when he saw Mr King at the presentation?* It made him feel even more guilty. He may have been afraid Mr King would realise he had cheated and say something.

    - *What dilemmas does Danny face when he is given the envelope?* Whether to accept the prize. Whether to own up to cheating.

    - *How does Danny hope to put things right?* He gives the prize away.

    - *What effect does the opening sentence have?* The reader realises that there was a dilemma and that Danny chose not to feel guilty. The reader may start to judge him.

    - *What evidence is there to tell you how Danny is feeling?* Mum tried to *drag* Danny...; "I've seen it before," he *muttered*; he pretended to have a tummy ache; Danny *trudged* behind her; ...but the 'rock' in his stomach hit a new low; his voice was small and croaky; suddenly his voice was clear and strong.

Independent, pair or guided work

- In pairs, the children read *Bad Girls* (Resource Page A), discuss and make notes.

Plenary

- Take some feedback.

Hot-seating Characters

Objectives

We will learn to give and accept responses during hot-seating, helping us to understand how people might feel when faced with a dilemma. We will also write a vivid description about how a character is feeling

You need: Resource Pages B and F.

Whole class work

- Tell the children you are going to take on the role of a character who is faced with a dilemma about cheating in a test. Tell them you are 'in the hot seat' and they can ask you any questions about the event and how you are feeling. Remind them you will answer as if you are that character.

- The children ask questions. Ensure your answers include a vivid account of how 'you' are feeling.

> My heart is racing. Will I get caught? The palms of my hands are sticky with perspiration.

> I feel terrible. My body feels like there is a big weight piled on top of it. I can't look at my teacher. I bow my head and look at the floor and want to run out of the room.

- If necessary, stop and tell the children that your character chose to cheat. Go back into character and describe feeling guilty.

- Give the children three minutes each to hot-seat with their partners how it feels to be jealous of a friend's new toy and/or scared because you are about to meet some bullies.

- Display Resource Page B and ask the children to identify the character's feelings. *How do you know she was feeling that?*

- Count the different ways that the writer has described the character's feelings. Some are about how her body *feels*, others are about the way her body *moves* and others about what the character is *thinking*.

Independent, pair or guided work

- The children write a paragraph (in the first person) describing how they are feeling in a given situation and ensuring they describe how their body feels, how they are moving and what they are thinking.

Plenary

- Share some work covering a variety of feelings. *Can everyone else identify the feeling?*

- Add these three aspects of description to the class checklist (see Resource Page F for ideas).

Writing the Introduction

Objective

We will write the introduction of a story about a dilemma, describing the feelings of the character vividly

You need: Resource Page C.

Whole class work

- Read the introduction to the story *Friends?* (Resource Page C).

- *How is the character feeling?* Answer: guilty.

- The children identify any features from the class checklist.

- Point out that the story is written in the first person. **Why do you think this is?** Answer: to make the reader feel more involved with the character. It's more personal.

- *Note that it is also written in the present tense and that the character had already faced a dilemma and has chosen to act in some way, but the readers do not yet know what this was. This means that some of the rest of the story is going to be a flashback and that bit will therefore be in the past tense.*

- *Why do you think I haven't written what the character is feeling guilty about yet?* Explain that you are trying to 'hook your readers' by making them want to read on to find out.

- Leave the model text on display so that each part can be added to it, ensuring the children always have access to a good model. Point out that they can use your model as a framework for their own story.

Independent, pair or guided work

- The children write the introduction to their own story, describing their character's feelings but trying to hook their readers by not letting on what the character has actually done.

Plenary

- Share some work using the response sandwich to evaluate: one good comment, one idea for improvement, another good comment.

Introducing Characters

Objective

We will introduce two main characters into our story, setting the scene for the issue that it raises

You need: Resource Page D.

Whole class work

- Review character plans from the previous lesson.

- Display and read the modelled character introduction (Resource Page D).

- *How does Joe describe himself? How does this affect the way readers feel about him? What does Joe think about his family?*

- The children identify features from the class checklist: varied sentence length, person, tense.

- Show how you have put in information that sets the scene for the issue (jealousy) and forthcoming dilemma.

> Joe's family is poor and his dad has left home but Edward's family is rich and his dad is still there. Also Edward is kind and Joe's only friend. Joe feels guilty for feeling jealous of Edward.

- Point out (if not already mentioned) that you still haven't told the reader what your main character has done. You are still trying to keep your reader hooked.

Independent, pair or guided work

- The children introduce two main characters to their story and set the scene for an issue to be raised.

Plenary

- The children read their work to response partners who should respond on the clarity and whether the writer has used features from the checklist.

- The children will need to make any suggested improvements in the light of the plenary and then copy up this section, adding it to the final copy of their introduction.

Using Flashbacks

Objective

We will write the build-up of our story as a flashback, identifying the issue but not the dilemma

You need: Resource Pages E and F.

Whole class work	• Display and read the story build-up (Resource Page E). • Ask the children to comment, referring to the class checklist (also see Resource Page F). • Point out that the story is in the past tense. Explain that this is because the character is telling you about something that happened in the past. ***This is called a flashback. Can you think of any books or films that use a flashback?*** (For example, the most recent *Star Wars* films are extended flashbacks. Flashbacks are often used in 'whodunnit' detective stories.) • Explain that flashbacks have to have a point. They should explain current events or why the character is behaving in such a way. In this example the flashback is the start of the explanation of why Joe is feeling so bad in the introduction. • Also note that as the writer you have still not given away the dilemma. The reader is now sure that the issue is jealousy but not what the jealousy drove Joe to do. Ask for suggestions about what Joe might have done.
Independent, pair or guided work	• The children write the main build-up of their story as a flashback, ensuring the issue is clear but not alluding to the specific dilemma faced by the character.
Plenary	• Share a couple of the build-ups asking the children to respond using a response sandwich – one good thing, one idea for improvement, a second good thing – and referring to the checklist.

111

(**Pupil copymaster**)

Bad Girls

They were going to get me. I saw them the moment I turned the corner. They were half way down, waiting near the bus stop. Melanie, Sarah and Kim. Kim, the worst of all. I didn't know what to do. I took a step forward, my sandal sticking to the pavement. They were nudging each other. They'd spotted me. I couldn't see that far, even with my glasses, but I knew Kim would have that great big smile on her face. I stood still. I looked over my shoulder. Perhaps I could run back to school? I'd hung around for ages already. Maybe they'd locked the playground gates? But perhaps one of the teachers would still be there? I could pretend I had a stomach ache or something and then maybe I'd get a lift in their car?

"Look at Mandy! She's going to go rushing back to school. Baby!" Kim yelled.

She seemed to have her own magic glasses that let her see right inside my head. She didn't wear ordinary glasses, of course. Girls like Kim never wear glasses or braces on their teeth. They never get fat. They never have a silly haircut. They never wear stupid baby clothes.

If I ran back they'd only run after me. So I went on walking, even though my legs were wobbly. I was getting near enough to see them properly. Kim was smiling all right. They all were. I tried to think what to do. Daddy told me to try teasing them back. But you can't tease girls like Kim. There's nothing to tease her about. Mum said just ignore them and then they'll get tired of teasing.

They hadn't got tired yet. I was getting nearer and nearer. My sandals were still sticking. I was sticking too. My dress stuck to my back. My forehead was wet under my fringe.

Jacqueline Wilson, in Moonlight, Seas and Chocolate Trees

❑ What issue does this story raise?

❑ Which is the main character in it? Why do you think the writer chose to write about this person?

❑ Does the opening sentence hook you? What question does it raise for the reader?

❑ Highlight parts of the story in which the main character faces a dilemma.

❑ Highlight any questions that the writer makes directly to the reader (rhetorical questions).

❑ 'So I went on walking, even though my legs were wobbly.' What does this sentence tell you about how the character was feeling?

❑ What does the final paragraph tell you about how the character was feeling?

❑ Why do you think the writer sometimes uses very short sentences?

Classworks Literacy Year 4 © Sue Plechowicz, Nelson Thornes Ltd 2003

(Exemplar material)

Describing feelings

As I pressed myself against the wall making my body as flat as possible, I could feel the cold, hard stone digging into me. It made me shiver despite the fact that my face was burning and my clothes were sticking damply to my skin. I could hear the blood roaring in my ears like the pounding of waves against the rocks. My heart was racing, thumping in my chest like a hammer while my legs were so weak and wobbly that I couldn't believe they were still holding me up.

He must be getting closer. The memory of his sneering laughter echoed in my head.

Menacing footsteps.

Closer … Louder …

I stood as still as a statue. Holding my breath, I closed my eyes. Maybe he wouldn't be able to see me either. Perhaps I should make a run for it. I'm much smaller and thinner than him so I should be able to run faster. Shouldn't I?

NOTES

<u>Way body feels</u>: shiver, face burning, clothes sticking, blood roaring in ears, heart racing, legs weak and wobbly

<u>Way character moves</u>: pressed as flat as possible, stood still as statue

<u>What character is thinking</u>: couldn't believe legs holding, perhaps I should run, smaller and thinner

<u>Use of similes</u>: blood roaring … like the pounding of waves; heart thumping … like a hammer; still as a statue

<u>Varied sentence length</u>

Friends? – story introduction

I just couldn't help myself; now I'm feeling dreadful. I have a strange ache in my tummy that feels like something is in there gnawing at me. I feel sick. Every time I think about what I have done, I can feel my face burning red. Red for embarrassment. Red for the devil! Surely only the devil would be so mean to a friend, wouldn't he? All I want to do now is to hide. Curl myself into a ball and make myself as small as possible. How could I have been so mean to my best friend?

Friends? – character introduction

My name is Joe. Most of the time I'm a pretty good guy, I guess, but I don't have a lot of friends because I have to dash straight home from school every day. I can't hang around like most of the other guys. They all bring their skateboards to school and hide them in the bike sheds during the day. They're not meant to bring them really but no one seems to bother as long as they don't start skating until they get to the end of the school road. I haven't got a board. My mum says she'll try and get me an old one from the second hand shop for my birthday but that's ages away. We haven't got much money. Not since Dad left me, my Mum and my brother and sister. They're younger than me and I have to take them home from school every day.

"Hold Jenny's hand tight," Mum says. "Don't forget, you're the oldest so you must look after the others."

How I hate being the eldest!

I do have one mate though. He's called Edward and he can't play after school either. His mum picks him up every day in their shiny, brand new BMW. Lucky Edward!

There's only him; no annoying little brothers or sisters to worry about. Edward's family is very rich, his dad is a doctor at the big hospital in town.

I sit next to Edward in class and play with him at break times. He doesn't seem to mind when Jenny comes up bothering us, crying because she wants Mum. Or when Sam, my grotty little brother, wants to share some of Edward's sweets. He just smiles, laughs and gives him loads!

Yes, Edward's my best friend; my only friend really. So how could I have done it to him?

(Pupil copymaster)

Friends? – story build-up

It all started the week before Edward's birthday. I know his family is very rich so I suppose I should have guessed that they'd throw him a party but I thought he'd only invite me, his only friend. So what a shock I got that Monday when he dashed into school, all smiley and excited, and ran straight up to Steven 'Sports Star' Simpson.

Steven 'Sports Star' is the most popular boy in our class. Everyone follows him around like puppy dogs; they think he's just wonderful. Just because he's a whiz on his skateboard. He can do every stupid trick there is apparently.

Steven looked a bit surprised too when he received his invitation. Everyone seemed to stop what they were doing and watch what he would say. Would he sneer at Edward and screw it up? But he didn't. No, he grinned from ear to ear, patted Edward on the back, and bellowed, "Thanks mate, I'd love to come."

I watched Edward breathe a sigh of relief and then hand out loads more invitations. To everyone in the class, in fact.

All this time I had a funny feeling in my stomach. I wanted to shout at Edward. Why was he bothering with all of them when he had me?

Finally, Edward gave me my invitation. I mumbled a quick thank you, shoved it into my pocket without opening it, and shuffled off into the cloakroom.

By the time the 'Big Day' came on Friday, I was so fed up with Edward and his new 'friends' going on about his rotten party that I really didn't want to go at all. In the morning I tried telling Mum how ill I was feeling. I moaned about having a stomach ache.

"Don't be silly," she laughed, quickly pushing the birthday card and present into my backpack. "You'll be fine when you're out in the fresh air. It's just excitement!"

I think she really thought that I didn't want to go to the party because I was ashamed of the present. It was a set of second hand Superman comics she'd found at the charity shop and my card was homemade. Actually, I knew Edward would be really thrilled with them because he collects comics and I'd ditch the card on the way to school! No, I really did feel ill. My stomach had been churning for days. Perhaps it was because I felt so let down and angry with Edward. I was supposed to be his only friend, wasn't I?

When we all piled out of Edward's BMW and the taxis Edward's parents had organised to get us to the party, I wasn't feeling any better. When I saw his huge pile of presents I felt even worse. I know I should have been happy for Edward but I just couldn't bring myself to be.

(Exemplar material)

Checklist for stories that raise issues

Structure

- Introduction

- Build-up of problem/issue

- A dilemma

- Resolution of dilemma

- Ending linked back to introduction

- Varied length sentences

- Cliffhanger

Language features

- Focus on describing characters feelings: the way body feels, the way they move, thoughts

- Involve reader by:
  - using first person
  - present tense or flashback in past tense
  - rhetorical questions
  - show dilemma by using 'perhaps' or 'maybe'

(**Marking ladder**)

Name: _____

Pupil	Objective	Teacher
	My story has: • an introduction which sets the scene • a build-up of problem/issue • a dilemma shown by words like 'perhaps' or 'maybe' • a resolution and ending linked back to the intro.	
	My story involves the reader by using: • present tense • first person • rhetorical questions.	
	I have focused on describing feelings.	
	I have hooked the reader with a cliffhanger.	
	I have varied the length of my sentences.	
	What could I do to improve my story next time?	

Newspapers and Reports

Outcome

A report for a class newspaper (compiled in ICT lessons); a non-chronological report; discussion and prediction of stories from headlines

Objectives

Sentence

1 to reread own writing to check for grammatical sense (coherence) and accuracy (agreement); to identify errors and to suggest alternative constructions.

2 to develop awareness of how tense relates to purpose and structure of text; to understand the term 'tense' (i.e. that it refers to time) in relation to verbs and use it appropriately.

5 to practise using commas to mark grammatical boundaries within sentences; link work on editing and revising own writing.

Text

16 to identify different types of texts, e.g. their content, structure, vocabulary, style, lay-out and purpose.

17 to identify features of non-fiction texts in print and IT, e.g. headings, lists, bullet points, captions which support the reader in gaining information efficiently.

18 to select and examine opening sentences that set scenes, capture interest, etc.; pick out key sentences/phrases that convey information.

19 to understand and use the terms 'fact' and 'opinion'; and to begin to distinguish the two in reading and other media.

20 to identify the main features of newspapers, including lay-out, range of information, voice, level of formality, organisation of articles, advertisements and headlines.

21 to predict newspaper stories from the evidence of headlines, making notes and then checking against the original.

24 to write newspaper-style reports, e.g. about school events or an incident from a story, including: composing headlines; using IT to draft and lay out reports; editing stories to fit a particular space; organising writing into paragraphs.

27 to write a non-chronological report, including the use of organisational devices, e.g. numbered lists, headings for conciseness by: generalising some of the details; deleting the least important details.

Speaking and listening

- to plan, predict and explore using discussion and group interaction.

Planning frame

- Investigate types and contents of newspapers.

- Investigate the features of recount texts and write a recount of a school event (or one linked to a history topic).

- Predict stories from headlines and write own headlines.

- Investigate the features of non-chronological texts and write a report linked to World War Two.

- Identify fact and opinion in the letters pages of newspapers.

Note

- Some of the reports could be used as part of an ICT project to write a class newspaper. This could also include work undertaken in different curricular areas, as well as poems, stories and playscripts written in other literacy blocks. This would give parents an overview of the outcomes in many areas of the curriculum and be a celebration of the children's work.

How you could plan this unit

Day 1	Day 2	Day 3	Day 4	Day 5
Reading Investigate newspapers. Types: daily/weekly, tabloid/broadsheet, Features: columns, headlines, photos, captions, articles, reports, editorials, sport, letters, classified	**Reading and analysis** *Identifying Features*	**Reading and analysis** Focus on introduction of recount. Set scene by answering five 'W' questions. The children identify these in opening paragraphs	**Reading** Headlines. Language: brief, play on words, alliteration. Add to checklist. The children discuss headlines and predict stories. They match up stories with their headlines in plenary	**Writing** Use texts from Day 2 and model alternative headlines (see Resource Page K). The children suggest headlines for newspaper report

Day 6	Day 7	Day 8	Day 9	Day 10
Reading and analysis Identify the language features of a recount text using texts from Day 2	**Writing** *Using Commas*	**Writing** *Chronological Order*	**Writing** *Writing in the Past Tense*	**Writing** Model conclusion of recount and evaluate using marking ladder (Resource Page L). The children write and evaluate own conclusions

Day 11	Day 12	Day 13	Day 14	Day 15
Reading and analysis *Non-chronological Reports*	**Reading and research** *Doing Your Research*	**Writing** Model writing non-chronological report on women at war referring to checklists. The children write own reports	**Writing and evaluating** Model evaluating report using marking ladder (Resource Page M). The children complete reports and evaluate	**Reading** Look at 'Letters to Editor' section of newspaper. Discuss 'fact' and 'opinion'. In pairs, the children identify these in other newspapers

Identifying Features

Objective

We will identify the structural features of recount texts by investigating newspaper reports

You need: Resource Pages A, B and K; OHT of a report from a local newspaper, plus class set of copies; whiteboards.

Whole class work

- Introduce the genre of recount text and its purpose: to retell events; to inform; to entertain.

- Explain that recount texts come in a variety of forms. In pairs, the children brainstorm examples: biography, magazine article, science investigation, an event in a history book, sports report, newspaper report and so on.

- *We are going to focus on newspaper reports, but all recount texts would have the same structure and language features. Today we are going to look at the structural features.*

- Display the enlarged copy of a newspaper report.

- Read through the text and invite the children to voice what they have noticed about the structure, using the exemplar analysis of a report for guidance (Resource Page A). Start a structure checklist (see Resource Page K for ideas).

- Identify that the first paragraph (often in a larger font) sets the scene by telling you who did it, what they did, when they did it, where it happened and often why it happened. These are the five W questions.

- Briefly, go through each of the five Ws, asking the children to find the answer to each question in the text.

- Point out that the main body of the text retells what happened in detail, in chronological (time) order. You may also wish to use the term 'linear' to describe how the report is structured.

- *Finally, there is a closing statement which brings the writing to a conclusion. Often there is a short, punchy last line.*

Independent, pair or guided work

- In pairs, the children read a newspaper report, identifying and highlighting the features from the checklist and underlining the five Ws.

Plenary

- Display a blank planning frame based on Resource Page B. *This frame represents the structure of a recount text. We can use a frame like this to help us when we write our own recounts. I am going to show you how our shared text fits on the frame.*

- Display the completed planning frame of your shared text and talk it through.

Using Commas

Objectives

We will write the introduction of a recount, using structural and language features we have identified in our reading. We will use commas to separate clauses

You need: Resource Pages C and D; strips of paper (at least five per child); whiteboards.

Whole class work

- Tell the children that they are going to be writing their own recount text, about a school event or visit. Explain that you are going to help them by modelling a recount text about Anne Frank – who wrote an important account of her life during World War Two.

- *Today we are going to write the introduction.*

- On the enlarged planning frame (Resource Page C) point out the five W answers.

- *Now I have the information but I need to put it all together in one sentence to form the introduction. Because there are five bits of information, I will need to find a way to separate them into meaningful chunks or the sentence will be too difficult to read. Can anyone tell me how I can separate the information?* Answer: by using commas.

- Choose five children to come to the front and hold up one of the strips of paper with a chunk of information (Resource Page D). Ask your class to suggest the order they should stand in to ensure that the sentence makes sense.

- Write commas and a full stop on whiteboards and invite more children to come and hold them up to separate the chunks. Other children can write other words they may want to use (for example, connectives) on other whiteboards.

- Demonstrate that the chunks can be used in several different orders, and clarify the use of commas.

- Collaborate on which order you think is best and write it down.

Independent, pair or guided work

- In pairs, the children use their own planning frame to record five Ws for a recount of a school event.

- In pairs, the children write chunks on strips of paper and manipulate them until they have found at least two different ways of writing the introduction. Ensuring that they use commas where appropriate, the children write out their introductory sentence at the top of a sheet of paper or in their notebooks, to be added to at a later date.

Plenary

- Share some introductory sentences. *Have the five Ws been addressed?*

Chronological Order

Objective

We will write the main events of our recount text in chronological order

You need: Resource Pages C, E and K; whiteboards.

Whole class work

- Explain that today everyone is going to be planning the main events section of their recount text.

- Look at checklist 1 (Resource Page K) and review that events should be in chronological order.

- Point to the vertical lines on the planning frame (Resource Page C). *These stand for each new event or piece of information.* Remind the children that they can add extra lines if necessary.

- Brainstorm events in Anne Frank's life and record on the board.

1. Born Germany 12/6/29
2. 1933 Nazis took power, moved to Amsterdam
3. 1940 Nazis took over Holland
4. 13th birthday, diary, Kitty
5. July 1942 annexe
6. 4th Aug 1944 arrested
7. Died Bergen-Belsen Oct 1944

- Explain that you will only be using the most important key events for the vertical lines on the timeline because details can be added between the lines.

- Ask individual children to write one key event on their whiteboard (or write them out yourself on separate boards). Then ask the children to come to the front and organise themselves in the correct order to make a human timeline.

- Model writing these key events on the vertical lines of the planning frame, and then add details between the lines (Resource Page E).

Independent, pair or guided work

- The children brainstorm their chosen event on their whiteboards, picking the key events and writing them on to their planning frame in time order. Add relevant details between the lines.

Plenary

- Ask the children to talk through their plan with their response partner. *Does it make sense?*

Writing in the Past Tense

Objective

We will write the main body of our recount text, paying careful attention to the tense and person and rereading to check for grammatical sense

You need: Resource Pages E, F and K; whiteboards.

Whole class work

- Explain that everyone is going to turn their plan of the main body of events into a written text, to follow on from the introduction written in a previous lesson.

- Look at the language features on checklist 1 (Resource Page K) and remind the children about verb tense. Ask the children to write some examples of past tense verbs on their whiteboards.

- Next remind the children that their text should be written in the third person. Ask them to write examples of third person pronouns on their boards. *You must keep writing in the same tense and person all the way through. To help you do this, reread each sentence to check as you go along.*

- Model how to turn the timeline plan (Resource Page E) into real text (Resource Page F), thinking aloud and referring to the checklist. Show that each horizontal line starts a new paragraph, which can be padded out with the details written between the lines.

- When you have finished, point out the time connectives that you have used to link the paragraphs.

Independent, pair or guided work

- The children write the main body of their recount underneath their introduction.

Plenary

- Share some work with the class. *Have they kept tense and person consistent?*

Non-chronological Reports

Objective

We will identify features of non-chronological texts

You need: Resource Pages G–I and K.

Whole class work

- Introduce the genre of non-chronological reports and its purpose: to describe the way things are or were.

> The word 'chronological' comes from the Greek:
> 'chronos' = time; 'logos' = word

- Explain that non-chronological reports can also be found in newspapers and more often, in magazines, and that although they are also called reports, they are very different from chronological reports. *The main difference is that, as the full name states, non-chronological reports are not in chronological order – not in 'time' order.*

- Display the planning frame below. Ensure the children recall that newspaper recount reports have a frame that is based on a timeline. *In this report the planning frame is circular, which shows that the information on it can be written in any order.* Refer back to the use of the term 'linear' to describe newspaper reports earlier in this unit.

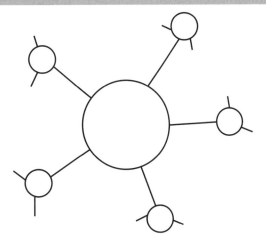

- Display the extract on persecution (Resource Page G). After reading through, ask the children to identify any structural or language features they have spotted (see Resource Page H). Add features to a class checklist (see Resource Page K for ideas).

Independent, pair or guided work

- In pairs, the children identify features in the text on air raid shelters (Resource Page I). *Could this be written in chronological order?* Elicit that some of the events take place at the same time.

Plenary

- *Did you find the same features? Have you found any different ones?*

- *Did anyone spot that all the texts we have looked at are history reports that obviously have to be in the past tense? However, all other non-chronological texts will be in the present tense. Why do you think this might be the case?*

Doing Your Research

Objective

We will research and plan a report on how World War Two affected children

You need: Resource Page J; non-fiction books on World War Two; access to the Internet; three large pieces of paper.

Whole class work

- *Today you are going to be writing reports on the effect that World War Two had on the lives of children in Britain.*

- Brainstorm what the children know, including background information from fiction books. Record their comments on a spidergram (Resource Page J).

- Organise information into categories and record these on a second spidergram. Demonstrate how you have grouped the information to make it easier to read at a glance.

- Divide the children into groups and allocate each group a category to research. Leave one category to model in the following lesson.

Independent, pair or guided work

- The children research their category using books or the Internet.

> USEFUL INTERNET SITES FOR HISTORY RESEARCH
>
> http://www.bbc.co.uk/history/forkids
>
> http://www.schoolhistory.co.uk
>
> http://www.activehistory.co.uk
>
> SEARCH ENGINES
>
> http://www.ask.co.uk
>
> http://www.google.com

- Bear in mind that Internet sources will bring up large numbers of 'hits'. With the children, practise refining the data to be entered.

- The children record their findings in note form on a spidergram.

Plenary

- On large pieces of paper, draw a spidergram for each category. Ask the children to provide some facts to put on each one.

- Leave these pinned up on the walls where the children can add new facts to them throughout the day. These can also be used as a plan by the children who did not manage to find sufficient facts for themselves.

(Exemplar analysis)

Example of analysis of *Poems, Pictures and Plops of Rain*

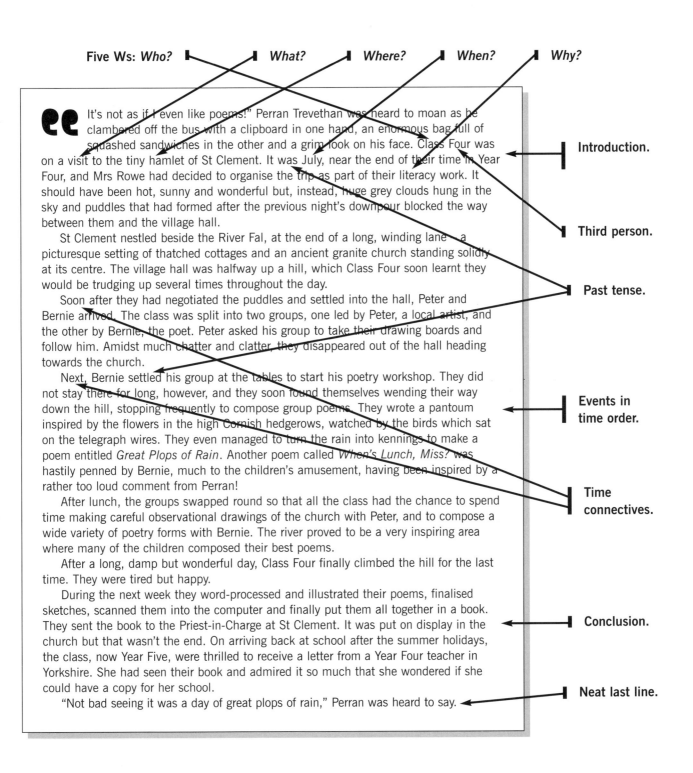

Five Ws: *Who?*   *What?*   *Where?*   *When?*   *Why?*

"It's not as if I even like poems!" Perran Trevethan was heard to moan as he clambered off the bus with a clipboard in one hand, an enormous bag full of squashed sandwiches in the other and a grim look on his face. Class Four was on a visit to the tiny hamlet of St Clement. It was July, near the end of their time in Year Four, and Mrs Rowe had decided to organise the trip as part of their literacy work. It should have been hot, sunny and wonderful but, instead, huge grey clouds hung in the sky and puddles that had formed after the previous night's downpour blocked the way between them and the village hall.

St Clement nestled beside the River Fal, at the end of a long, winding lane, a picturesque setting of thatched cottages and an ancient granite church standing solidly at its centre. The village hall was halfway up a hill, which Class Four soon learnt they would be trudging up several times throughout the day.

Soon after they had negotiated the puddles and settled into the hall, Peter and Bernie arrived. The class was split into two groups, one led by Peter, a local artist, and the other by Bernie, the poet. Peter asked his group to take their drawing boards and follow him. Amidst much chatter and clatter, they disappeared out of the hall heading towards the church.

Next, Bernie settled his group at the tables to start his poetry workshop. They did not stay there for long, however, and they soon found themselves wending their way down the hill, stopping frequently to compose group poems. They wrote a pantoum inspired by the flowers in the high Cornish hedgerows, watched by the birds which sat on the telegraph wires. They even managed to turn the rain into kennings to make a poem entitled *Great Plops of Rain*. Another poem called *When's Lunch, Miss?* was hastily penned by Bernie, much to the children's amusement, having been inspired by a rather too loud comment from Perran!

After lunch, the groups swapped round so that all the class had the chance to spend time making careful observational drawings of the church with Peter, and to compose a wide variety of poetry forms with Bernie. The river proved to be a very inspiring area where many of the children composed their best poems.

After a long, damp but wonderful day, Class Four finally climbed the hill for the last time. They were tired but happy.

During the next week they word-processed and illustrated their poems, finalised sketches, scanned them into the computer and finally put them all together in a book. They sent the book to the Priest-in-Charge at St Clement. It was put on display in the church but that wasn't the end. On arriving back at school after the summer holidays, the class, now Year Five, were thrilled to receive a letter from a Year Four teacher in Yorkshire. She had seen their book and admired it so much that she wondered if she could have a copy for her school.

"Not bad seeing it was a day of great plops of rain," Perran was heard to say.

Introduction.

Third person.

Past tense.

Events in time order.

Time connectives.

Conclusion.

Neat last line.

Planning frame for *Poems, Pictures and Plops of Rain*

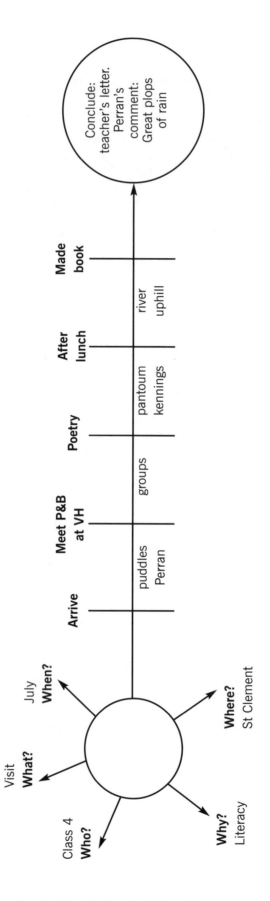

(Exemplar material)

Anne Frank – plan for introduction

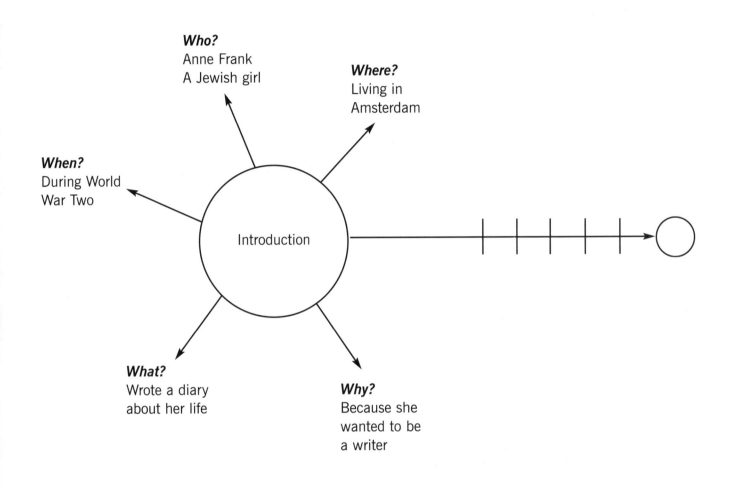

Who?
Anne Frank
A Jewish girl

Where?
Living in
Amsterdam

When?
During World
War Two

Introduction

What?
Wrote a diary
about her life

Why?
Because she
wanted to be
a writer

Classworks Literacy Year 4 © Sue Plechowicz, Nelson Thornes Ltd 2003

Pupil copymaster

Information on Anne Frank

during World War Two
a Jewish girl called Anne Frank
wrote a diary
that tells us about her experiences
living in Amsterdam

Exemplar material

Anne Frank – timeline plan

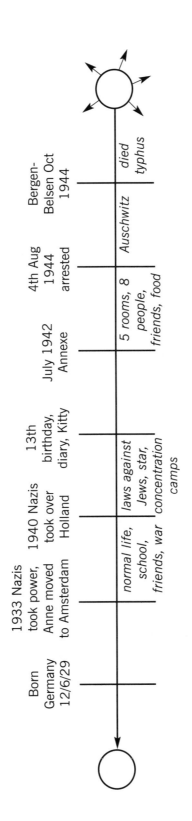

Born Germany 12/6/29

1933 Nazis took power, Anne moved to Amsterdam

normal life, school, friends, war

1940 Nazis took over Holland

laws against Jews, star, concentration camps

13th birthday, diary, Kitty

July 1942 Annexe

5 rooms, 8 people, friends, food

4th Aug 1944 arrested

Auschwitz

Bergen-Belsen Oct 1944

died typhus

(**Pupil copymaster**)

Anne Frank recount

Anne Frank, a Jewish girl living in Amsterdam during World War Two, wrote a diary which tells us about her experiences.

Anne was born in Germany on 12th June 1929. Her parents were called Edith and Otto and she had a three-year-old sister called Margot.

In 1933, the National Socialist (Nazi) party took power in Germany. The leader of the Nazis, Adolf Hitler, hated Jews and treated them very badly so Otto Frank moved his family to Amsterdam in Holland to get away from them.

In Holland Anne and Margot led a happy life. Anne had lots of friends and was very popular. However, in 1940 the Nazis invaded Holland and passed many laws against the Jews. All Jews had to wear a yellow star on their clothes. Then news came from Germany that the Nazis had started to kill Jews using poison gas.

Meanwhile, on her thirteenth birthday, in 1942, Anne was given a diary by her parents. Anne loved writing. She treated the diary like her best friend, calling it 'Kitty'.

A few weeks later, Margot was sent a letter saying that she was to be sent to a German work camp. Rather than let this happen to Margot, the Frank family went into hiding in a secret annexe above Otto Frank's offices. Another Jewish family also hid there. The annexe consisted of five small rooms, one toilet and a washbasin. The entrance to it was hidden behind a heavy bookcase. Friends who worked in the offices risked their own lives by sneaking food into them but the families had to be very careful not to make any noise during the daytime in case other people heard and told the Nazis they were there.

Anne was not able to take many things to the annexe with her but she did take Kitty, her diary. The family stayed hidden for two years and during that time, Anne wrote down all her thoughts and feelings in it. She also realised that she wanted to become a writer and she started to write short stories.

Sadly, on 4th August 1944 someone did betray them. The Nazis found the annexe and the Franks were sent to a Dutch concentration camp. A month later, Anne, Margot and Edith were moved to another camp in Auschwitz, Poland. They never saw Otto again.

Then, in October 1944, Anne and Margot were moved to Bergen-Belsen concentration camp in Germany. By this time, both girls were seriously ill. They had caught typhus, a disease caused by the terrible conditions they were forced to live in. In March, Margot died. Anne died a few days later.

Otto Frank was the only survivor of the family. After the end of the war, some friends gave him Anne's diary. They had found it in the secret annexe. Otto allowed the diary to be published so that others could understand how it felt to be a Jew during World War Two.

Anne's wish to become a writer had come true and her diary has become, for many people, a symbol of the millions of Jews who were murdered by the Nazis.

Persecution

PERSECUTION means being punished for what you believe. Ever since Judaism began, Jews have been persecuted because of their beliefs. No one really knows why. One reason is probably because keeping their religion and their own way of doing things has always been important for Jews. Some people may have been frightened of them. Some people have not understood what Jews believe.

PERSECUTION BY THE NAZIS

The worst persecution of the Jews happened when the Nazis ruled Germany in the 1930s and 40s. Their leader, Adolf Hitler, believed that people with blond hair and blue eyes were better than everyone else. He began to persecute many other groups.

Not liking somebody because of religion or the colour of their skin is called **prejudice**. Hitler was prejudiced against Jews. He made laws that said Jews could not do things like own shops or cars, or go to school. The list went on and on. Then the Nazis decided to get rid of Jews completely. Soldiers went from one house to the next, asking if there were any Jews there. Any Jews found were taken away. Anyone found hiding Jews was killed.

The Jews who were taken away were taken to special camps. They were treated very badly in these camps. They were not given enough food or clothes, and all their hair was shaved off. Many were killed straight away. Others died from illness or from lack of food.

By the end of the Second World War in 1945, six million Jews had died. This was one Jew out of every three Jews alive in the world. Six million is a number too big to imagine: it is like one in ten of all the people in Britain today, or every person in London.

Sue Penney, in Judaism

(Exemplar analysis)

Example of analysis of *Persecution*

Present tense (except for historical parts).

Introduction: definition; explains what text is about.

Description in categories (non-chronological). Moves from general to specific.

Paragraph 2: Nazis (general).

Paragraph 3: prejudice.

Third person.

Technical words.

Paragraph 4: Nazis (specific).

Conclusion.

PERSECUTION means being punished for what you believe. Ever since Judaism began, Jews have been persecuted because of their beliefs. No one really knows why. One reason is probably because keeping their religion and their own way of doing things has always been important for Jews. Some people may have been frightened of them. Some people have not understood what Jews believe.

PERSECUTION BY THE NAZIS

The worst persecution of the Jews happened when the Nazis ruled Germany in the 1930s and 40s. Their leader, Adolf Hitler, believed that people with blond hair and blue eyes were better than everyone else. He began to persecute many other groups.

Not liking somebody because of religion or the colour of their skin is called **prejudice**. Hitler was prejudiced against Jews. He made laws that said Jews could not do things like own shops or cars, or go to school. The list went on and on. Then the Nazis decided to get rid of Jews completely. Soldiers went from one house to the next, asking if there were any Jews there. Any Jews found were taken away. Anyone found hiding Jews was killed.

The Jews who were taken away were taken to special camps. They were treated very badly in these camps. They were not given enough food or clothes, and all their hair was shaved off. Many were killed straight away. Others died from illness or from lack of food.

By the end of the Second World War in 1945, six million Jews had died. This was one Jew out of every three Jews alive in the world. Six million is a number too big to imagine: it is like one in ten of all the people in Britain today, or every person in London.

Sue Penney, in Judaism

(Pupil copymaster)

Air raid shelters

In 1939, when war was about to break out, the British Government realised that they had to do something to protect people from air raids so they granted permission to build air raid shelters in or near homes, schools and public buildings.

Public Shelters

Many brick-built surface communal shelters were constructed and the basements of public buildings were strengthened. Schools built large shelters in their playgrounds. In London, people began to use the underground stations as shelters.

Anderson Shelters

The Home Secretary, Sir John Anderson, organised for portable shelters to be delivered to people with gardens in the areas most likely to be attacked. These consisted of six curved sheets of corrugated steel that had to be bolted together to form a tunnel. This was buried in the garden, over a metre deep, and then earth was piled on the top. They could protect up to six people and were often lined with bunk beds. However, these shelters, known as 'Andersons', were cold and damp with often only a candle to light them. They were very unpopular.

Morrison Shelters

More popular were Morrison shelters. These looked like huge steel tables with wire mesh on the sides and a mattress underneath. They were used inside so families could settle down onto the mattress each night and not have to go outside in the cold when there was an air raid.

During the war, over a million homes were destroyed by bombs. The air raid shelters saved the lives of many people. Many of these shelters have survived and can still be seen in gardens today.

Classworks Literacy Year 4 © Sue Plechowicz, Nelson Thornes Ltd 2003

(Exemplar material)

Spidergrams for World War Two

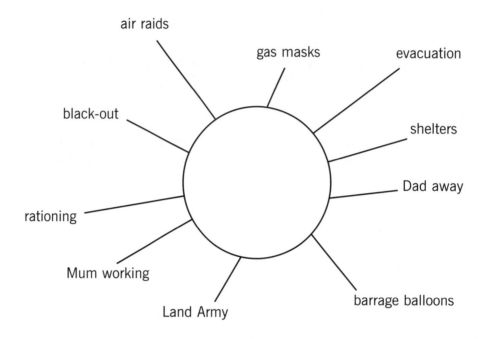

air raids

gas masks

evacuation

black-out

shelters

Dad away

rationing

Mum working

Land Army

barrage balloons

1. Brainstorm

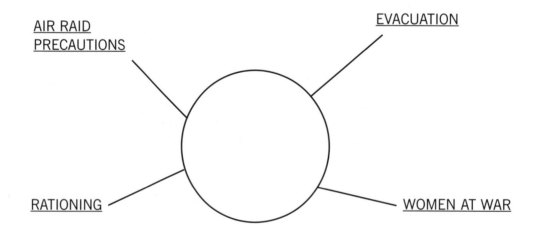

AIR RAID
PRECAUTIONS

EVACUATION

RATIONING

WOMEN AT WAR

2. Categories

Classworks Literacy Year 4 © Sue Plechowicz, Nelson Thornes Ltd 2003

(Exemplar material)

Checklists and model for newspapers and reports

Example of a checklist for newspaper-style writing ①

Structure

- Introduction sets the scene with the five Ws

- Events are recounted in chronological order

- A closing statement concludes the article

- A neat last line grabs attention

Language features

- Past tense

- Third person

- Time connectives

Example of a checklist for a non-chronological report ②

Structure

- Introduction gives general description

- Specific information is organised in categories

- A closing statement brings writing to a conclusion.

Language features

- Present tense or past if historical report

- Third person

- Technical words

Example of modelling alternative headlines ③

PUDDLES ARE NO DETERRENT TO CLASS FOUR!

INCLEMENT WEATHER FOR POETS IN ST CLEMENT

RAIN DOESN'T STOP YEAR FOUR'S PLAY

HAMLET INSPIRES YOUNG WRITERS

Classworks Literacy Year 4 © Sue Plechowicz, Nelson Thornes Ltd 2003

(Marking ladder)

Marking ladder for a newspaper-style report

Name: _____

Pupil	Objective	Teacher
	My introduction sets the scene with the five Ws.	
	I have recounted events in chronological order.	
	My closing statement brings the writing to a conclusion.	
	It has a neat last line to grab attention.	
	It is in the past tense.	
	I have used the third person.	
	I have linked paragraphs using time connectives.	
	What could I do to improve my report next time?	

(Marking ladder)

Marking ladder for a non-chronological report

Name: _____

Pupil	Objective	Teacher
	My introduction includes a general description about what is to follow.	
	I organised my report in specific categories.	
	I ended with a conclusion.	
	I used the present tense (or past tense for historical report).	
	I used the third person.	
	I used technical words.	
	What could I do to improve my report next time?	

Stories about Imagined Worlds

Outcome

Fantasy settings making use of expressive and descriptive language

Objectives

Sentence

1 to revise and extend work on adjectives from Y3 term 2 and link to work on expressive and figurative language in stories and poetry – constructing adjectival phrases.

Text

1 to understand how writers create imaginary worlds, particularly where this is original or unfamiliar, such as a science fiction setting and to show how the writer has evoked it through detail;

2 to understand how settings influence events and incidents in stories and how they affect characters' behaviour;

3 to compare and contrast settings across a range of stories, to evaluate, form and justify preferences;

4 to understand how the use of expressive and descriptive language can, e.g. create moods, arouse expectations, build tension, describe attitudes or emotions;

5 to understand the use of figurative language in poetry and prose; compare poetic phrasing with narrative/descriptive examples; locate use of simile;

10 to develop use of settings in own writing, making use of work on adjectives and figurative language to describe settings effectively;

13 to write own examples of descriptive, expressive language based on those read. Link to work on adjectives and similes.

Planning frame

- Discuss features of fantasy stories and investigate their settings.

- Investigate the type of language used to create atmosphere.

- Use the framework of a setting in *The Hobbit* as a plan for own writing.

- Experiment with expanding adjectives to similes and compressing similes into adjectival phrases.

- Use setting to impart something about character.

How you could plan this unit

Day 1	Day 2	Day 3	Day 4	Day 5
Reading and analysis	**Reading and analysis**	**Writing** Review checklist. Model how to use Tolkien's setting to write your own (Resource Page F). The children do the same	**Writing** Identify adjectives and adjectival phrases in the Harry Potter excerpt. Change adjectives into comparative similes. The children rewrite passage using similes to describe nouns. Plenary: similes are effective but don't overuse	**Writing** Focus on similes. Compress into adjectival phrases. The children experiment with compressing other similes. Plenary – adjectives, similes and compressed adjectival phrases make effective description – vary use
Fantasy Features	*Fantasy Settings*			

Day 6	Day 7	Day 8	Day 9	Day 10
Reading and writing Settings can tell you about characters. Hobbits are sociable, tidy, vain, fond of food, probably fat. Model an extension of your story setting (Resource Page F) including hints about characters	**Writing**	**Writing**	**Writing** Go through modelled text from Day 8. Ask the children to identify features from the checklist. The children read own work to partners and use response sandwich. Re-draft as necessary	**Evaluation** Evaluate work using marking ladder (Resource Page H). Share with class
	Effective Language	*Effective Writing*		

Fantasy Features

Objective

We will recognise some of the features writers use in stories set in imagined worlds

You need: Resource Pages A, B and G.

Whole class work

- Introduce the genre of stories about imagined worlds. Discuss the term 'fantasy' to describe things that are imagined or unreal. Brainstorm examples: *The Lord of the Rings*; *The Hobbit*; Harry Potter books; Narnia books; Star Wars series and so on.

- *What things would you expect to find in a fantasy story?* Answer: magic; extraordinary or impossible events; made-up words, names and places; dragons, elves, fairies, wizards and so on.

- Differentiate between fantasy stories that are set in the real world (Harry Potter, Buffy, Narnia stories) and those which are not set on earth or at this time (Star Wars, Star Trek), but explain that all are still in the fantasy genre.

- *Where might fantasy stories be set?* Answer: magical forests; parallel worlds; outer space; the future.

- Point out that the setting can be to do with *place* and *time*. Add to the class checklist (see Resource Page G for ideas).

- Read *Lothlorien* (Resource Page A). The children close their eyes and try to build a picture of the place in their heads.

- *What features indicate the text is from a story about an imagined world?* Answer: magic; elves; fairies; made-up places/words.

- Explain that this is a setting from *The Lord of the Rings*. **The main feature of this text is that there are a lot of made-up words.** Focus on some of them in turn and ask the children to describe to their response partner what picture the words evoke in their heads.

Independent, pair or guided work

- In pairs, the children identify and highlight features in *The Abradizil* (Resource Page B) that indicate a fantasy setting.

Plenary

- Share findings and write features on to the checklist.

- *Which setting do you prefer – Lothlorien or Abradizil? Why?*

142

Fantasy Settings

Objective

We will recognise some of the language features writers use in stories set in imagined worlds, and understand how expressive and descriptive language can create atmosphere

You need: Resource Pages C, D and G; whiteboards; paper; coloured pencils or paint.

Whole class work	• *Writing the setting for a story is about building a picture in the reader's head. This is especially important when the story is set in an imagined world because the reader has little or no prior knowledge about that world.*
	• Explain that you are going to read two versions of the same setting. Read the extract on Resource Page C but miss out some details, description and adjectives. Ask the children if they can picture the classroom in their heads. Then read the whole extract and ask the same question.
	• Discuss what it was about the second text that allowed them to build up a much clearer picture. Answers should include:
	– adjectives
	– powerful verbs
	– alliteration.
	• Ask the children to identify adjectives used to describe the room or items in the room and write them on their whiteboards. For example, ***What adjectives have been used to describe the light?*** Answer:

dim   crimson

Discuss how the atmosphere would change if the adjectives were 'bright' and 'yellow'. Repeat for various descriptions.

• Establish that adjectives are not only used to build a picture but also to create an atmosphere. In this case the atmosphere is magical and mysterious. Add to the class checklist (see also Resource Page G).

Independent, pair or guided work	• Read the extract from *The Hobbit* (Resource Page D), then the children draw or paint a picture of the hobbit-hole.
Plenary	• *Has everybody drawn similar pictures?* Discuss similarities and differences.
	• Establish that this writer (Tolkien) used adjectives in conjunction with similes, to give a really detailed description and, as a consequence, most readers will have built up a similar picture in their heads.

round … like a porthole

tubeshaped … like a tunnel

• Again, ask which of today's settings the children prefer and why.

Effective Language

Objective

We will rewrite a setting making it more effective by using features from the checklist

You need: Resource Pages E and G.

Whole class work

- Remind the children that a good setting paints a picture in the reader's head. Look at the class checklist (see also Resource Page G) and establish that in order to do this it needs to:
  - describe the place (where)
  - give the time (when)
  - build up an atmosphere and hint about characters by using effective language
  - describe what can be heard, smelt, touched and so on.

- Display the top half of Resource Page E, a bland description. Model rewriting and improving the setting, ensuring that you have included a description of what can be seen, heard, smelt or possibly touched, referring to the checklist.

- In pairs, the children suggest choices of effective language.

Independent, pair or guided work

- The children improve the following setting for themselves, referring to the checklist.

> Jane opened the door. There was a field. It was full of poppies. In the middle of the field there was a tree. Jane walked to it and noticed it had a hole in the trunk. Above the hole there was something carved in the wood. Jane could hear a noise.

Plenary

- Share some work, asking the children to evaluate and state preferences using a response sandwich: one good comment; an idea for improvement; another good comment.

Effective Writing

Objective

We will write an event in a fantasy setting, making use of effective language

You need: Resource Pages F and G; the children's settings written in previous lesson.

Whole class work

- Explain that you are going to use the setting you have written and add the next few paragraphs in which:
  - the main character enters
  - he or she moves through the setting
  - he or she finds something important and unexpected in the setting.

- Model the writing (Resource Page F), referring to the checklist (Resource Page G). As you write, invite comments and ideas from your class.
  - *What do you think might happen next?*
  - *What would you write here?*
  - *What would be a good adjective to use here?*

Independent, pair or guided work

- The children write their next paragraph, adding a 'problem' for the main character using their own setting from a previous lesson.

- The children who find this difficult could brainstorm ideas with their response partner.

Plenary

- Share some work. *Have they remembered to include a description of what can be seen, heard, smelt and touched and other features of the checklist?*

- Choose one of the more powerful descriptions and, with your class, analyse why it is successful.

(Pupil copymaster)

Lothlorien

Just east of the Misty Mountains, beside the Silverlode, which flows into the Great River Anduin, lies Lothlorien – the Golden Wood – the fairest Elf-kingdom remaining in Middle-earth.

Lothlorien is the home of the Wood Elves, who are almost invisible to visitors to the wood they guard, as they move swiftly and silently through the tree canopy, camouflaged by their magical grey cloaks. Throughout the Golden Wood grow the towering mallorn trees, the tallest and most beautiful trees in Middle-earth.

In the grass of the forest floor bloom the golden stars of elanor and pale white flowers of the niphredil. The silver pillars of the mallorns tower up into a splendid canopy of golden leaves, in the many-levelled branches of which the Elves build their flets: their dwellings, or high houses.

At the heart of the Golden Wood lies Caras Galadhon, the city in which the Lord Celeborn and Lady Galadriel have their royal hall, a magnificent flet, nestled high in the crown of the mightiest mallorn of all.

from The Lord of the Rings – The Fellowship of the Ring
Visual Companion, *by Jude Fisher*

(**Pupil copymaster**)

The Abradizil

It all happened a very long time ago, in a very strange city, in a very distant land. The city was built on the banks of a river. When the morning sun was shining, it shone on hundreds of towers and spires and domes, and set them all sparkling with light. But the buildings beneath them were dark. The streets were narrow and small. The houses were crammed together, at crazy angles, in untidy rows. Their walls were peeling and crumbling, and their roofs sagged. They had lots of little rooms in them that bulged outwards, like bumps. It was a strange city, all right – a strange, bent, rather sinister city, and some strange, bent, rather sinister creatures lived there: magicians, wizards, goblins, dwarfs. The city was ruled by a sinister man, as well, whose name was Horg. You wouldn't have wanted to live in this city. But Franz lived there.

from The Abradizil, *by Andrew Gibson, in* Moonlight, Seas and Chocolate Trees

Classrooms

In fact, it didn't look like a classroom at all; more like a cross between someone's attic and an old fashioned teashop. At least twenty small, circular tables were crammed inside it, all surrounded by chintz armchairs and fat little pouffes. Everything was lit with a dim, crimson light; the curtains at the windows were all closed, and the many lamps were draped with dark red scarves. It was stiflingly warm, and the fire which was burning under the crowded mantelpiece was giving off a heavy, sickly sort of perfume as it heated a large, copper kettle. The shelves running around the circular walls were crammed with dusty-looking feathers, stubs of candles, many packs of tattered playing cards, countless silvery crystal balls and a huge array of teacups.

from Harry Potter and the Prisoner of Azkaban, *by J.K. Rowling*

Pupil copymaster

The Hobbit

In a hole in the ground there lived a hobbit. Not a nasty, dirty, wet hole, filled with the ends of worms and an oozy smell, nor yet a dry, bare, sandy hole with nothing in it to sit down on or to eat; it was a hobbit-hole, and that means comfort.

It had a perfectly round door like a porthole, painted green, with a shiny yellow brass knob in the exact middle. The door opened on to a tube-shaped hall like a tunnel; a very comfortable tunnel without smoke, with panelled walls, and floors tiled and carpeted, provided with polished chairs, and lots and lots of pegs for hats and coats – the hobbit was fond of visitors. The tunnel wound on and on, going fairly but not quite straight into the side of the hill – The Hill, as all people for many miles round called it – and many little round doors opened out of it, first on one side and then on another. No going upstairs for this hobbit: bedrooms, bathrooms, cellars, pantries (lots of these), wardrobes (he had whole rooms devoted to clothes), kitchens, dining rooms, all were on the same floor, and indeed on the same passage. The best rooms were all on the left-hand side (going in), for these were the only ones to have windows, deep-set round windows looking over his garden, and meadows beyond, sloping down to the river.

from The Hobbit, *by J.R.R. Tolkien*

(Exemplar material)

Modelling rewriting a description

Jane looked around. The garden was enclosed by a wall and had flowerbeds running along the edges. There were lots of trees swaying in the breeze with grass growing underneath them. In the wall at the far end of the garden there was a door with a key sticking out of the lock.

Improved description

Jane looked around. The garden was totally enclosed by an ancient ivy-clad wall. On top of the wall stone dragons stared down at Jane, seeming to watch her every move. Along the edges of the garden there had once been flowerbeds but now they were overgrown, full of weeds and vicious-looking brambles with shark-fin thorns. Jane could smell honeysuckle but she couldn't see it. Perhaps the brambles had smothered that too. Trees stood on guard, their branches bending over like witches' fingers ready to snatch at Jane. They swayed in the summer breeze, creaking like old bones. Underneath, the grass grew in tangled, unkempt knots. In the wall at the far end of the unloved, forgotten garden there was a wooden door. It had a large metal ring for a handle and a huge, rusty key was sticking out of the lock.

(Exemplar material)

Modelled writing

On that day, the Griffle sensed he would be needed. Something in the air whispered to him and he could smell trouble in the Enchanted Forest today. He quickly stored some superberries in a pouch and filled another with icy-cold water from the stream. Silently he made his way to the clearing. At first he kept himself hidden behind one of the largest of the Mumbles' trees but after a while the sound of a Mimble crying reached his ears and he hurried out across the clearing and into the forest beyond.

Mimbles rarely cried, he knew that. Even when they tumbled out of their dens in the tree branches or scraped their knees on hedgehog spines, they didn't cry. They were brave little fellows. The Griffle was very concerned. Suddenly the crying stopped but this only concerned him more. If something had happened that was so bad it made a Mimble cry then he knew of nothing in this world would stop it so abruptly.

All at once the Griffle found himself face to face with a creature he never thought he would actually set eyes on himself. It was a little girl! She was sitting among the leaves on the forest floor, cradling a motionless Mimble in her arms. The Mimble had a huge cut on his forehead and his eyes were closed.

(Exemplar material)

Checklist and models for stories about imagined worlds

Example of a checklist for a fantasy setting (1)

Structure

- Set in an imaginary place or time

- Describe what can be seen, heard, smelt and/or touched

- Have make-believe characters such as elves, dragons, wizards and so on

- Use special effects such as magic

- The setting should tell something about characters

Language

- Use made-up words

- Use adjectives and adjectival phrases to create atmosphere

Example of a modelled setting (2)

In a forest there lived a Griffle. Not a spooky, fearsome forest filled with devilish demons nor a plain ordinary forest with nothing but trees and squirrels: it was an enchanted forest and that means fun!

It had a magical meeting place in a clearing with trees swaying in the breeze and magnificent Mumbles sitting on their elegant branches while Mimbles played happily below.

Example of a modelled setting that hints at character (3)

The Griffle had made his home in a cave beside the sparkling stream that meandered its way through the forest. He had chosen the cave because it was hidden by thick superberry bushes. He could creep out for fresh clear water and collect nuts and herbs without anyone even noticing he was there. He could also gather and store the magical healing superberries when they first ripened, long before the mischievous Mimbles had had time to use them for berry-ball fights or berry-ball kicking matches.

Classworks Literacy Year 4 © Sue Plechowicz, Nelson Thornes Ltd 2003

Marking ladder

Name: _____

Pupil	Objective	Teacher
	My story is set in an imaginary place or time.	
	It describes what can be seen, heard, smelt and/or touched.	
	There are make-believe characters such as elves, dragons, wizards and so on.	
	I used special effects such as magic.	
	The setting tells something about the characters.	
	I used some made-up words.	
	I used adjectives and adjectival phrases to create atmosphere.	
	What could I do to improve my story next time?	

Stories in Series

Outcome

A book (with the story in chapters) for a younger audience

Objectives

Sentence

2 to use the apostrophe accurately to mark possession through:

- identifying possessive apostrophes in reading and to whom or what they refer;

- understanding basic rules for apostrophising singular nouns, e.g. 'the man's hat'; for plural nouns ending in 's', e.g. 'the doctors' surgery' and for irregular plural nouns, e.g. 'men's room', 'children's playground';

- distinguishing between uses of the apostrophe for contraction and possession beginning to use the apostrophe appropriately in own writing.

4 to recognise how commas, connectives and full stops are used to join and separate clauses; to identify in their writing where each is more effective.

Text

3 to understand how paragraphs or chapters are used to collect, order and build up ideas.

9 to recognise how certain types of texts are targeted at particular readers; to identify intended audience.

12 to collaborate with others to write stories in chapters, using plans with particular audiences in mind.

13 to write own examples of descriptive, expressive language based on those read. Link to work on adjectives and similes.

14 note-making: to edit down a sentence or passage by deleting the less important elements, e.g. repetitions, asides, secondary considerations and discuss the reasons for editorial choices.

Planning frame

- Identify features of stories for younger children.

- Locate chapter breaks in a story outline, plan story and draw storyboard.

- Listen and respond to others' story plans.

- Write and illustrate a story with four chapters.

- Focus on commas, connectives and apostrophes.

- Use note-making skills to write a story blurb.

Note

- This unit is linked to Stories about Imagined Worlds, page 140.

How you could plan this unit

Day 1	Day 2	Day 3	Day 4	Day 5
Reading and analysis	**Analysis and planning**	**Drawing and planning** Draw storyboard. Two drawings per chapter (each child draws four pictures)	**Speaking and listening** Model talking through own story plan, ask for feedback and amend. The children do same with own story and new partner	**Writing**
The Target Reader	*Planning Chapters*			*Chapter 1*

Day 6	Day 7	Day 8	Day 9	Day 10
Writing	**Writing** The children collaborate on chapter 3	**Writing** Display and read Resource Page H. Review how ending links back to story beginning. The children collaborate on final chapter	**Writing** Use of commas and connectives to make complex sentences from simple ones. Use examples from the children's stories. The children do the same.	**Writing**
Chapter 2				*Apostrophes*

Day 11	Day 12	Day 13	Day 14	Day 15
Writing The children help you mark your model story using marking ladder, then mark their own stories	**Writing** Word-process final copy of stories, leaving space for illustrations (1 per chapter). Make into a book	**Writing and illustrating** Illustrate stories and front covers	**Writing**	**Reading** Share stories with Year 1 or 2. Laminate covers so books can become part of school library
			A Book Blurb	

The Target Reader

Objective

We will recognise how texts are targeted at particular readers, and identify features of stories targeted at younger audiences

You need: Resource Page H; a selection of storybooks suitable for children in Year 1 and 2 (at least 3 books for each group of 6); a big book fantasy story borrowed from Year 1 or 2; whiteboards.

Whole class work

- Display the big book text and ask the children to scan through the title and first page and identify the genre. Answer: fantasy.

- Read the book and ask the children to record on whiteboards all the features that indicate that it is a fantasy story (see Stories About Imagined Worlds, page 140).

- *Who do you think this story was written for?* Answer: younger children.

- *How did you know it was for younger children?* Establish that it has:

> a simple story line
>
> talking animals — or fairies?
>
> illustrations
>
> simple but interesting language

Start to compile a class checklist (see Resource Page H for ideas).

- Explain that the outcome of the unit will be to write a book for a younger child, but in order to do so you need to be sure about what features these books have in order to hook your audience.

Independent, pair or guided work

- The children scan through/read a selection of books for younger children, noting key features.

Plenary

- *Did the books have similar features to the main text? Did you find any other features to add to our checklist?*

- Discuss what other audiences the librarian in your school would have to consider when buying new stock. For example who would read junior horror stories? Pet or horse stories? Harry Potter? Picture books?

Planning Chapters

Objectives

We will learn how chapters are used to build up ideas. We will also collaborate on a plan for a story for a younger child, in detail, from an outline

You need: Resource Pages A and B; whiteboards; children's work from the unit on Stories About Imagined Worlds, page 140.

Whole class work

- Explain that the children are going to work in pairs to plan their story following an outline.

- Review what a story hill frame looks like. The children draw it on their whiteboards. Then display Resource Page A.

- Read through Resource Page B.

- Tell the children that the story they are going to write needs to be in chapters. Explain that, for a simple story, new chapters could start when there is a *change of setting* or a *new event*.

- In pairs, the children discuss where they think the end of the first chapter would be. (Allow 1 minute.)

- Establish that it will be after the introduction of the main characters and the setting: 'A girl … finds a door.' Mark this on the outline (Resource Page A) beside *Introduction of characters and setting*.

- Explain that you are going to use the setting and characters you wrote about in the unit on Stories About Imagined Worlds and that when the children plan their own stories they need to choose one or both of their settings also.

- Model your own plan for each chapter of your story.

Independent, pair or guided work

- In pairs, the children begin to plan their own story from the outline written in the unit on Stories About Imagined Worlds. *What are the main points to go in each of the four chapters? How are the settings going to be fitted in?*

Plenary

- Share some plans, asking the children to evaluate by referring to the checklist and using a response sandwich: one good comment; one idea for improvement; another good comment.

Chapter 1

Objectives

We will write chapter 1 of a story for younger children, collaboratively. We will use descriptive and expressive language and write in paragraphs

You need: Resource Page C.

Whole class work

- Read your modelled chapter 1 (Resource Page C) to the children.

- Ask the children to comment. Point out that you have ended the chapter by using a 'fiction hook'. You are trying to 'hook' readers by making them want to find out what is behind the door. Add this to your class checklist.

- You could use the example of Charles Dickens' serial writing, magazine writing, or comics to introduce the idea of 'instalments'. Fiction hooks make the reader want to buy the magazine the next week to see what happens.

- Explain that when you word-processed the story, you forgot to put it in paragraphs. Ask the children to suggest where each paragraph should start and mark text accordingly using //. Draw attention to:

  > new idea
  >
  > change of focus
  >
  > change of time or place

Independent, pair or guided work

- In pairs, the children write their own first chapter, from plans, in paragraphs. Chapters should end with a 'fiction hook'.

Plenary

- Ask the children to report back about how they organised working in a pair. Did they pick a scribe or did they each take turns? What was successful/caused problems? Discuss how these could be resolved.

- Encourage both children to take ownership of the work by photocopying it each day so that each child has a copy for their file and for use in subsequent lessons.

Chapter 2

Objective

We will write chapter 2 of a story for younger children collaboratively, using paragraphs

You need: Resource Page D; children's work from the unit Stories About Imagined Worlds, page 140.

Whole class work

- Display and read your modelled chapter 2 (Resource Page D).

- Invite the children to comment, referring to your class checklist.

- Review writing a fantasy setting (checklist 1, page 152) and what sort of elements might be incorporated.

- Explain that the children will be starting their own chapter 2 with the description of a setting.

- The children can use their own work (description of a setting) but the following paragraphs should be written collaboratively. Thus, each child will have a slightly different story for their file.

Independent, pair or guided work

In pairs, the children write their own chapter 2.

Plenary

- Share some paragraphs in which the character finds the problem. *What sort of problems has the writer set their characters? What resolutions do you think might follow the problem?*

- Responses should refer to your class checklist and use a response sandwich: one good comment; one suggestion for improvement; a second good comment.

Apostrophes

Objective

We will show an understanding of how to use possessive apostrophes and apostrophes of omission

You need: Resource Page F; whiteboards; a large sheet of paper.

Whole class work

- Look at Resource Page F with your class. The children highlight all the words with apostrophes.

- *What are apostrophes?* The children should be able to tell you that they replace a letter to contract the word, but they may struggle to explain possessive apostrophes.

- Focus on each apostrophe of omission, asking the children to write on their whiteboards the letter(s) that the apostrophe replaces.

- If there are children who are not secure in their understanding of this, ensure that their independent task focuses on this.

- Move on to the words with apostrophes of possession. Explain that these mean 'belonging to' but that we use apostrophes to make the writing more economical. For example, 'The dog's bone' is much easier than 'The bone belonging to the dog'.

- *If you can't add 'belonging to' to the sentence because it doesn't make sense, then a possessive apostrophe is not required.*

- Ask the children to look at words with possessive apostrophes in the text and write out what belongs to whom on their whiteboards.

- On a large piece of paper, draw two columns headed *Omission* and *Possession*. Write words from the text in the appropriate columns.

Independent, pair or guided work

- The children check through their own stories, making sure that they have used apostrophes appropriately.

Plenary

- Collect and classify examples of apostrophes on a large sheet. Add words found to the class collection.

- Introduce 'its' and 'it's'. Explain that you only ever use an apostrophe of omission in this word, never an apostrophe of possession.

- For children struggling with this concept, explain that English is an 'untidy' language and that some rules and exceptions have to be learned rather than reasoned.

A Book Blurb

Objective

We will make notes by editing our story and use them to help us to write a book blurb

You need: Resource Page G.

Whole class work

- Explain to the children that you are going to make some notes about the main points of the story and then use some of them to help you write a blurb.

- Model note-making (see Resource Page G).

- Discuss what you would want to put in a blurb:

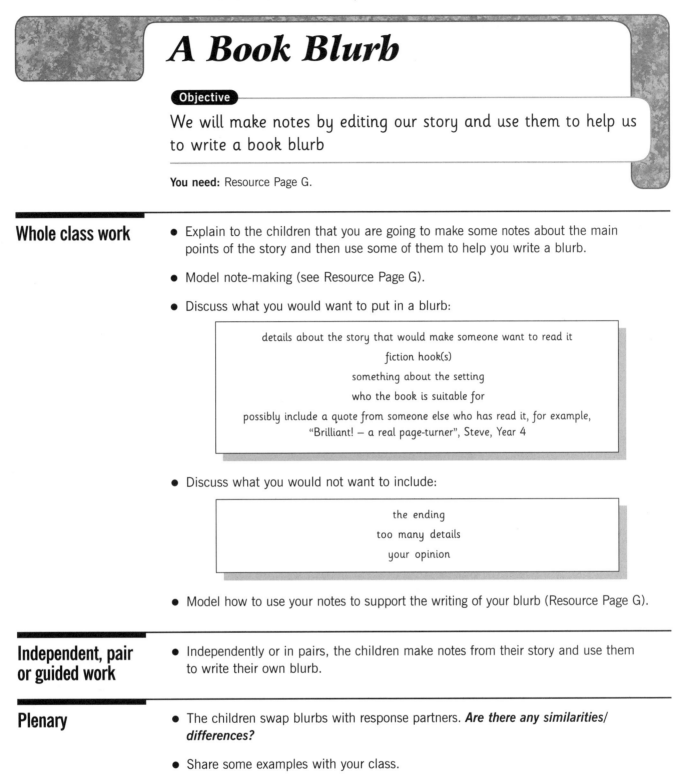

> details about the story that would make someone want to read it
>
> fiction hook(s)
>
> something about the setting
>
> who the book is suitable for
>
> possibly include a quote from someone else who has read it, for example, "Brilliant! – a real page-turner", Steve, Year 4

- Discuss what you would not want to include:

> the ending
>
> too many details
>
> your opinion

- Model how to use your notes to support the writing of your blurb (Resource Page G).

Independent, pair or guided work

- Independently or in pairs, the children make notes from their story and use them to write their own blurb.

Plenary

- The children swap blurbs with response partners. ***Are there any similarities/ differences?***

- Share some examples with your class.

(Exemplar material)

Modelled story frame

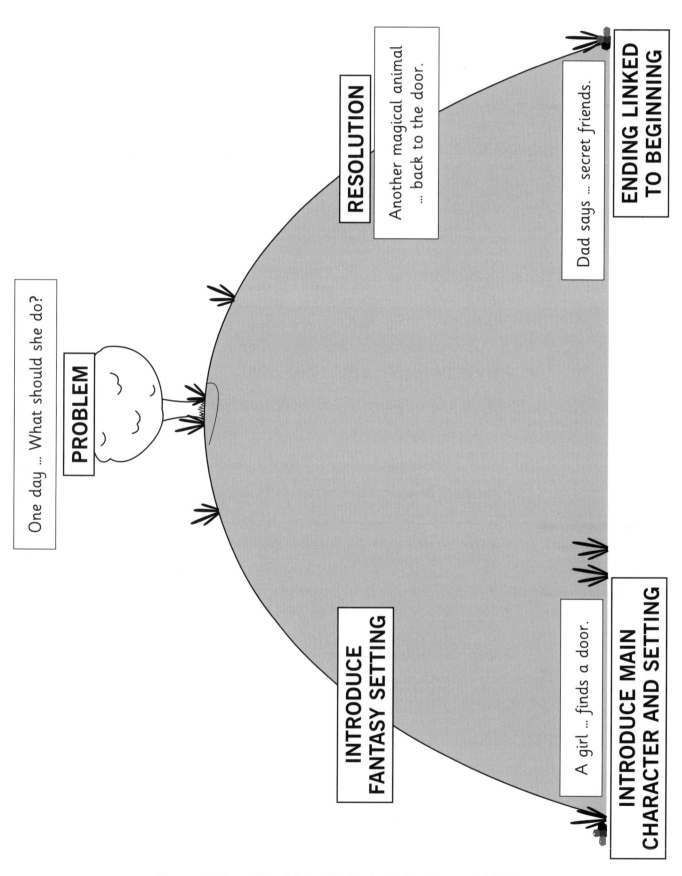

PROBLEM

One day ... What should she do?

RESOLUTION

Another magical animal ... back to the door.

ENDING LINKED TO BEGINNING

Dad says ... secret friends.

INTRODUCE FANTASY SETTING

A girl ... finds a door.

INTRODUCE MAIN CHARACTER AND SETTING

Classworks Literacy Year 4 © Sue Plechowicz, Nelson Thornes Ltd 2003

(Pupil copymaster)

Story outline

A lonely little girl, whose mum is in hospital, moves to a new house. The garden is large, overgrown and surrounded by high walls. In one of the walls the girl finds a door. One day the girl is bored. She decides to try and find out what is behind the door in the garden. When she opens the door she is transported into a magical place where she meets fantastic creatures. She hears a creature crying. The problem is that he is injured. What should she do? Another magical animal arrives and helps them. The girl makes friends with the animals. Then she hears a voice. It is her dad. The animals get her back to the door. Dad says he has a surprise for her. He shows her the surprise and the girl knows she will never be lonely again. She has her secret friends.

Pupil copymaster

Chapter 1

Tonya was feeling really sad and lonely. It was the beginning of the long summer holidays and she had just moved to a new house. What was even worse, her mum was in hospital and Tonya really missed her. Tonya's new garden was very large and overgrown. It was totally enclosed by an ancient ivy-clad wall. On top of the wall stone dragons stared down at Tonya, seeming to watch her every move. Along the edges of the garden there had once been flowerbeds but now they were overgrown, full of weeds and vicious-looking brambles with shark-fin thorns. Tonya could smell honeysuckle but she couldn't see it. Perhaps the brambles had smothered that too. Trees stood on guard, their branches bending over like witches' fingers ready to snatch at Tonya. They swayed in the summer breeze, creaking like old bones. Underneath, the grass grew in tangled, unkempt knots. In the wall at the far end of the unloved, forgotten garden there was a wooden door. It had a large metal ring for a handle and a huge, rusty key was sticking out of the lock. Tonya longed to have a friend to explore it with but all her friends lived a long way away now.

(Pupil copymaster)

Chapter 2

One day Tonya was feeling really bored. Her dad was busy decorating and didn't have any time to spend with her so she wandered out into the garden. She was beginning to like the garden more now and it didn't feel as spooky as it had at first.

After a while Tonya found herself by the old wooden door in the wall. The rusty key was still sticking out of the lock and today it was as if it was calling to her, daring her to turn it and open the door. Should she? At that moment Tonya decided that she would. Perhaps there was someone on the other side who could play with her.

Carefully, Tonya tried to turn the key. It wouldn't budge so she tried again using both hands. It squeaked, scraped and suddenly clicked around. She grabbed the metal ring, twisting it as hard as she could. The door creaked open.

Tonya peeped around the door and to her amazement there in front of her was a forest. Not a spooky, fearsome forest filled with devilish demons nor a plain ordinary forest with nothing but trees and squirrels; it was an enchanted forest and that means sparkling, silver trees and glittering golden bushes.

Tonya started to walk through the trees, hoping to find out what kind of creatures lived there. Everything was so beautiful she felt sure that they would be friendly. After a while she saw some rabbits hopping around a bush. Well, she thought they were rabbits but when she got closer she noticed they had fur the colour of candyfloss!

She was not at all surprised when one of the strange animals started to talk to her.

"Hello, Tonya, we wondered when you would visit us." Now Tonya was surprised. They knew her name! When she asked them how they knew it, the animals started to giggle and explained mysteriously that they were magical Mombles and they knew everything! Mombles, thought Tonya, how exciting!

"Who else lives in the forest?" she asked.

"Oh, loads of creatures. Mumbles are the oldest and wisest. They're a bit like your owls. Then there are the Mimbles. They're the naughtiest pixies you will ever see. They're always up to mischief!"

"Don't forget the Griffle!" another Momble chirped up. "You won't see much of him though. Keeps himself to himself does the Griffle."

Tonya was delighted. She couldn't wait to meet all these new fantastic creatures. She asked the Mombles to tell her more about the Griffle. He sounded particularly mysterious. The Mombles told her that the Griffle had made his home in a cave beside the sparkling stream that meandered its way through the forest. They thought he had chosen the cave because it was hidden by thick superberry bushes. He could creep out for fresh, clear water and to collect nuts and herbs without anyone even noticing he was there. He could also gather and store the magical healing superberries when they first ripened, long before the mischievous Mimbles had had time to use them for berry-ball fights or berry-ball kicking matches.

As she sat chatting to the Mombles all of a sudden a great howl was heard, followed immediately by noisy crying. "What on earth is that?" asked Tonya.

"Sounds like a Mimble to me," muttered one of her new friends. "Didn't I tell you they were always in trouble?"

"It sounds like they need help," said Tonya, jumping up and hurrying towards the pitiful cries.

Sure enough, when Tonya reached the crying she found a strange little pixie-like creature lying on the floor with blood gushing from a gash on his head.

"Help him, please help him," pleaded another worried-looking Mimble standing in a group nearby. Tonya sat beside the injured Mimble and gathered him into her arms. He stopped crying immediately but his head looked bad. What should she do?

Classworks Literacy Year 4 © Sue Plechowicz, Nelson Thornes Ltd 2003

(**Pupil copymaster**)

Chapter 3

What Tonya could do with was the Griffle and strangely enough, on that day, the Griffle had sensed he would be needed. Something in the air had whispered to him and he could smell trouble in the Enchanted Forest. He had quickly stored some of the superberries in a pouch and filled another with icy-cold water from the stream. Silently he'd made his way to the clearing. At first he kept himself hidden behind one of the largest of the Mombles' trees but after a while the sound of a Mimble crying reached his ears and so he hurried out across the clearing and into the forest beyond.

Mimbles rarely cried, he knew that. Even when they tumbled out of their dens in the tree branches or scraped their knees on hodgeheg spines, they didn't cry. They were brave little fellows. The Griffle was very concerned. Suddenly the crying stopped but this only concerned him more. If something had happened that was so bad it would make a Mimble cry, then he knew of nothing in this forest that would stop it so abruptly.

All at once the Griffle found himself face to face with a creature he thought he would never actually set eyes on himself. It was a girl! She was sitting amongst the leaves on the forest floor, cradling a motionless Mimble in her arms. The Mimble had a huge cut on his forehead and his eyes were closed. As the Griffle bent his huge head down towards the injured Mimble, Tonya and the other Mombles stared spellbound. He was such a beautiful creature, rather like a dragon, with glistening scarlet scales as red as rubies.

When Tonya found her voice she muttered desperately, "Can you help him?"
"Of course," replied the Griffle. "Just let me pour some of this water over the cut and then some drops of superberry juice. Hold him still, my dear."

As soon as the juice touched the Mimble's head the cut disappeared! Everyone gasped as the magic worked.

Very quickly the Mimble struggled out of Tonya's arms. Mimbles don't like to be cuddled. However, he was very wobbly on his feet and so the Griffle told his friends to take him home to rest. As the Mimbles left they called out to Tonya, "Come and play with us another day, Tonya. We'll have great fun!"

Tonya waved at them, then turned to smile at the Griffle.
"Thank you, Mr Griffle, you were magical."
The Griffle's cheeks turned an even deeper shade of crimson red and he huffed shyly at Tonya, "It was nothing, my dear."

Suddenly, Tonya heard a voice calling her name. It was her dad. "I must get back to my garden," she said.

"We'll show you the way," offered the Mombles and, as if by magic, Tonya was whisked back to the wooden door.

"I'll come again very soon," whispered Tonya but by then her new friends had hopped back into the Enchanted Forest.

(**Pupil copymaster**)

Chapter 4

Back in her garden Tonya found her dad.

"Ah, there you are, Tonya," he said. "Come quickly. There's a big surprise waiting for you back in the house."

Tonya wondered what the surprise could be. Her dad was very excited about something. He'd grabbed her hand and was speedily making his way along the overgrown path. He's going to trip over those roots if he's not careful, Tonya thought as they hurried on. Then I'll have to get the Griffle to help him, she thought, giggling to herself.

It wasn't long before Tonya saw what Dad was so excited about. As they got nearer to the house a figure could be seen in the doorway. It was Tonya's mum!

"Mum's home from hospital!" Tonya shouted.

"Yes, and look who's come home with her!" Tonya peered at her mum. In her arms, Mum was cradling a white bundle.

"Meet the newest member of our family, Tonya. It's your baby brother!"

Tonya was amazed. She stared at her brother's little red face. His big blue eyes stared back and at that moment Tonya knew she'd never be lonely again.

(Pupil copymaster)

Turning notes into a blurb for a book

1. Tonya is lonely because she has just moved into a new house and her mum is in hospital.

2. The house has a large, overgrown garden with a door hidden at the bottom.

3. Tonya finds an Enchanted Forest behind the door.

4. The forest is full of talking creatures: Mombles (pink rabbits), Mimbles (naughty pixies), Mumbles (wise birds) and a Griffle.

5. The Griffle is shy and doesn't like to mix with others. He is also a healer.

6. Tonya finds an injured Mimble but doesn't know how to help him.

7. The Griffle arrives and heals him with superberry juice.

8. Tonya goes home and finds Mum has come home too.

9. Tonya has a new baby brother.

10. Tonya won't be lonely any more because she has her brother and her magical friends.

Tonya is lonely. She has just left all her friends to move to a new house but before long she discovers the neglected, unloved garden holds the key to an enchanted world full of mysterious creatures.

Read about Tonya's first adventure in the Enchanted Forest where she meets the candyfloss Mombles, naughty, troublesome Mimbles and the mighty Griffle.

Is she in danger or will these magical creatures become the friends she is searching for?

(Exemplar material)

Checklist for stories in series

Structure

- Use a simple story line

- Include talking animals or fairies

- Start a new chapter when there is a change of setting or a new event

- End some chapters with a 'fiction hook'

- Start a new paragraph for each new idea

- Use illustrations

Language features

- Use simple but interesting language

- Use connectives and commas to extend simple sentences

(**Marking ladder**)

Name: _____

Pupil	Objective	Teacher
	My story has a simple story line.	
	My story has talking animals/fairies.	
	I started a new chapter for a change of setting or a new event.	
	Some of my chapters end with a 'fiction hook'.	
	I used paragraphs for each new idea.	
	I used illustrations.	
	I used simple but interesting language.	
	I used connectives and commas to extend simple sentences.	
	I used apostrophes correctly.	
	What could I do to improve my story next time?	

Explanations and Information Books

Outcome

A class wall chart on the course of a river; an explanation of the water cycle; a talk, using notes, about one of these

Objectives

Sentence

3 to understand the significance of word order, for example: some re-orderings destroy meaning; some make sense but change meaning; sentences can be re-ordered to retain meaning (sometimes adding words); subsequent words are governed by preceding ones;

4 to recognise how commas, connectives and full stops are used to join and separate clauses; to identify in their writing where each is more effective.

Text

15 to appraise a non-fiction book for its contents and usefulness by scanning, e.g. headings, contents list.

16 to prepare for factual research by reviewing what is known, what is needed, what is available and where one might search.

17 to scan texts in print or on screen to locate key words or phrases, useful headings and key sentences and to use these as a tool for summarising text.

18 to mark extracts by annotating and by selecting key headings, words or sentences, or alternatively, noting these.

19 to identify how and why paragraphs are used to organise and sequence information.

20 to identify from the examples the key features of explanatory texts:
   ● purpose: to explain a process or to answer a question
   ● structure: introduction, followed by sequential explanation, organised into paragraphs
   ● language features: usually present tense; use of connectives of time and cause and effect; use of passive voice
   ● presentation: use of diagrams, other illustrations.

21 to make short notes, e.g. by abbreviating ideas, selecting key words, listing or in diagrammatic form.

22 to fill out brief notes into connected prose.

23 to collect information from a variety of sources and present it in one simple format, e.g. wall chart, labelled diagram.

24 to improve the cohesion of written explanations through paragraphing and the use of link phrases and organisational devices such as sub-headings and numbering.

25 to write explanations of a process, using conventions identified through reading.

Speaking and listening
   ● to discuss and interact with others, accommodating different views, looking for consensus.

Planning frame

   ● Appraise books about rivers for their usefulness.

   ● Research questions about rivers in a variety of books.

- Take notes and produce a labelled class wall chart about the course of a river.
- Give a talk on rivers using notes.
- Investigate the features of explanation texts.
- Write an explanation on the water cycle.
- Prepare and carry out talk/assembly on the water cycle.

Note

- This unit is linked to Geography 'Rivers' and Science 'The Water Cycle'.

How you could plan this unit

Day 1	Day 2	Day 3	Day 4	Day 5
Reading Appraise a book on rivers for its content and usefulness by scanning. Note headings, contents list, text layout and other features. Discuss findings	**Reading** *Reviewing Knowledge*	**Reading and research** *Doing Research*	**Notetaking** Model taking notes. The children do the same for own research. In plenary, decide section drawings of rivers for each group and add to class wall chart	**Display work** Prepare drawing of river on large roll of paper. Model how to write up notes. Add to wall chart. In groups, the children do the same for own section

Day 6	Day 7	Day 8	Day 9	Day 10
Speaking and listening Using notes and writing from previous lessons, plan a talk about the course of a river for another class or invited guests	**Reading and analysis** *Structural Features*	**Reading and analysis** Share model text (Resource Page B) and identify language features (Resource Page C). The children analyse features in another text (Resource Page D)	**Research** **Why don't oceans overflow? Where does rain come from?** Model making notes. The children make notes for other sections on planning frame	**Writing** *Opening Statement*

Day 11	Day 12	Day 13	Day 14	Day 15
Writing *Using Connectives*	**Writing** Continue the sequenced explanation, focusing on use of paragraphs. Evaluate and redraft as necessary	**Writing** *Word Order*	**Writing** Focus on texts with additional information boxes. Model how to write one for own text (example 2, Resource Page H). The children write additional boxes for own explanation	**Writing** Model checking through and amending work, referring to checklists (Resource Page H). The children do the same and write up final presentation

Day 16	Day 17	Day 18	Day 19	Day 20
Writing Look at a glossary from an explanation text. Ensure the children's understanding of nature and purpose. Model writing glossary for own text (example 3, Resource Page H). The children add a glossary to own explanation	**Drawing** Show the children a diagram to support your explanation text. Discuss benefits of supporting diagrams. The children draw own diagram of the water cycle	**Evaluating** Model how to evaluate your explanation using the marking ladder (Resource Page I). The children do the same for own work. Share work	**Speaking and listening** Prepare a class assembly on the water cycle. The children work in groups, each taking a section of the cycle to talk about	**Assessment** To reinforce the cross-curricular nature of explanations and to assess the children's learning, ask them to write an explanation on a relevant Science or D&T topic

Reviewing Knowledge

Objective

We will prepare for research on rivers by reviewing what we know already and compiling questions we would like to find the answers to

You need: flip chart; whiteboards; books on rivers (at least one between three).

Whole class work

- Explain that, by the end of the week, the class will be producing a labelled wall chart on the course of a river for their Geography display. The children will be working in groups, with each group researching and providing information on a different section of the river.

- *First we need to review what we already know about rivers.*

- Divide the flip chart page down the middle. Head the columns:

What we already know	What we want to know

- Brainstorm and record suggestions on the flip chart. For example, if the children say they know that a river starts in the mountains and ends at the sea, a possible question could be: 'What is the name of the start of a river?' Include any words that they have heard and think are about rivers even if they don't know the exact meaning. The children may have heard of the word 'meander' but not know the exact meaning.

- Remind the children of their work on Day 1. *What kind of features may be helpful for finding out the answers you need and information you want to know?* Answer: contents lists, glossary, diagrams, sub-headings and so on.

- Explain that today you want them to scan books to get an idea about rivers. They don't necessarily have to find the answers to the things on the flip chart but should get an overview of the subject and what the books may be able to help them with when researching a specific section of the river.

Independent, pair or guided work

- In threes, the children scan through a book on rivers to get an idea about whether it will be useful for researching information about specific parts of a river.

- The children find at least one fact per group that they didn't know about a river and record on their whiteboards.

Plenary

- Share the new facts and record on the flip chart.

- *Have any of the questions been answered?*

Doing Research

Objective

We will begin to find out about rivers by selecting key headings, words or sentences about the features found in a specific section of a river

You need: a selection of books on rivers for each group.

Whole class work

- Review the flip chart work from the previous lesson.

- Explain that a river can be divided into three sections:

> where it starts – the upper course or young river
>
> the middle course or grown-up river
>
> where it ends – the lower course or old river

- Identify the three river sections pictorially, explaining that there are features that can be identified specific to each section.

- Divide a new flip chart sheet into five and give each a heading.

Upper Course	Middle Course	Lower Course	Work/Uses of a River	Additional Facts
Source	*Meanders*	*Mouth*	*Irrigation*	*Longest = Nile*
Mountain rivers	Ox-bow lakes	Delta	Dams	Erosion
Melting snow	Valley	Mud flats	Factories	Pollution
Streams	Flood plains	Tidal	Towns and cities	Holy River Ganges
Tributaries	Marsh lands	Estuary	Leisure	
Rapids	Grass lands		Transport	
Waterfalls				

Tell the children that you are going to give them one feature or keyword for each section and that they will research that section themselves.

- Divide the class into five groups and allocate them a river section or topic.

Independent, pair or guided work

- In groups, the children research their given topic, identifying key features in preparation for more detailed research and notetaking.

Plenary

- Add your findings to the class flip chart.

Structural Features

Objective

We will identify the structural features of explanation texts

You need: Resource Pages A–D and G; whiteboards.

Whole class work

- Explain that the texts your class has been looking at over the past week have been examples of explanation texts. *They have explained how rivers are formed.* Tell the children that they are going to continue studying explanation texts, identifying their features.

- *What do you think is the purpose of explanation texts?* Answer: they tell you how or why something works or happens.

- *Where can we find examples of explanation texts?* Answer: non-fiction books, for example in Geography, Biology and so on; Science text books; technical manuals, for example for a car or a washing machine; question and answer leaflets; science reports and so on.

- Show a blank version of the planning frame for an explanation text (Resource Page A) and ask the children to consider how the structure of the text you are going to share could fit on to it.

- Read Resource Page B, asking the children to note structural features on their whiteboards.

- Discuss the text and structural features (Resource Page C). Demonstrate that the planning frame is a flow chart (this happens, leading to this, which leads to this and so on).

- Write structural features on to a class checklist (see Resource Page G for ideas).

Independent, pair or guided work

- In pairs, the children identify and annotate the structural features of an explanation text (Resource Page D).

Plenary

- Ensure that the features were found by the children. Identify any others, for example a title in the form of a question, and add to your class checklist.

- *What could the writer have done or used to make this explanation clearer?* Establish that pictures or diagrams would have helped. Add this to your checklist.

Opening Statement

Objective

We will use notes to support writing the opening statement of an explanation of the water cycle

You need: Resource Pages A and E; whiteboards.

Whole class work

- Explain to the children that today you are going to write the opening statement of an explanation text.

- Go through your class checklist to review features.

- Write your title:

> How does an oxbow lake form?

Point out that this indicates what you are going to explain.

- Display your plan (Resource Page A) and then model how to fill out the notes to write the opening statement, omitting the question for the reader (Resource Page E).

- Ask the children to write on their whiteboards what they think you should write for the final sentence of your opening. Share their ideas. Establish that it should be a question (to engage the reader). Choose one of their ideas or write your own from the model and add to your text.

Independent, pair or guided work

- Using their planning frame notes as support, the children write the opening statement of their explanation of the water cycle.

Plenary

- Share some opening statements. *Have they used a question? Is it correctly punctuated? Does the statement make sense? Does it encourage the reader to want to know more?*

- Evaluate some opening statements using a response sandwich: one good comment; one idea for improvement; another good comment.

Using Connectives

Objective

We will use notes to support writing the main body of text for an explanation of the water cycle, with a focus on connectives

You need: Resource Page E; whiteboards.

Whole class work

- Explain that today you are going to write the main body of your explanation text on the water cycle.

- Review your class checklist. Establish that the main body of an explanation text consists of a series of logical steps and that each new step or idea should have a new paragraph.

- *How should I join the paragraphs together so that the whole text flows in an understandable way?* Answer: use time connectives.

- The children brainstorm some examples of time connectives and write them on their whiteboards. Jot a few of them on the edge of your plan and explain that these are to help you to remember to use them in the text.

- *What should I use to keep the sentences within the paragraphs flowing in a sensible way?* Answer: causal connectives. Again, the children brainstorm some examples.

- Write these two sentences on the board:

  > Once a river leaves the mountains and hills it reaches flatter land.
  >
  > It flows more slowly.

- Establish that the flatter land causes the river flow to slow and that you need a causal connective to join the two sentences together so that they also flow well together and make sense.

- Give the children one minute to discuss ways of connecting the sentences with their response partners.

- Record some of their answers and say that you will use one of them in your text.

- Using the notes on your plan, model the main body of your text (see Resource Page E). Ensure that you refer to language features on your class checklist throughout.

Independent, pair or guided work

- Using their planning frame notes to support their work, the children write the main body of their explanation of the water cycle, with a focus on connectives.

Plenary

- Share some work, asking the children to evaluate using a response sandwich and paying particular attention to the use of connectives.

177

Word Order

Objective

We will use notes to support writing the concluding statement for an explanation of the water cycle, with a focus on word order

You need: Resource Pages E and F; whiteboards.

Whole class work

- Explain that today you are going to write a concluding statement for your explanation text and that although you know what you want to say, you want to experiment with the order of the words to make the first sentence sound more interesting.

- Write these notes on the board:

> An oxbow lake is an abandoned meander.
>
> An oxbow lake is surrounded by fertile mud and silt.
>
> It is a very good place for plants and wildlife.

- *How could I combine the first two sentences?* Encourage the children to discuss with response partners. Answer:

> An abandoned meander or oxbow lake is surrounded by
> fertile mud and silt

- Hand out the sentence cards (Resource Page F) to selected children and ask them to arrange themselves into a human sentence. Work out all the different combinations. Ensure that the children understand that although the phrases and verbs can be rearranged, the actual nouns in the noun phrases cannot.

- Choose the most successful sentence and use it to start your model concluding statement.

- Then add your final sentence which relates the subject to the reader (final paragraph of Resource Page E).

Independent, pair or guided work

- Encourage the children to use their planning frame notes to support their writing of a concluding statement for their explanation text, with a focus on word order.

Plenary

- Share some work, focusing on word order and the different ways the children have related the subject to their readers.

- *Why do you think the writers of explanation texts use this technique?*

(Exemplar material)

Modelled plan for oxbow explanation

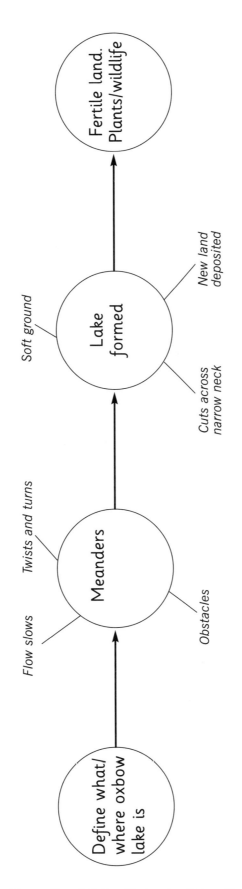

Fertile land.
Plants/wildlife

New land
deposited

Soft ground

Lake
formed

Cuts across
narrow neck

Twists and turns

Meanders

Flow slows

Obstacles

Define what/
where oxbow
lake is

(**Pupil copymaster**)

An explanation text

How a hovercraft works

Hovercraft carry people and goods over land and water. They travel across surfaces without actually touching them. How is this possible?

Hovercraft have rubber skirts around their bases. They usually have four engines, which drive four propellers and fans. The propellers look like those on aeroplanes, but they push the hovercraft forward rather than pulling it along. The fans pump air into the rubber skirt.

When a hovercraft is being loaded, the skirt is squashed almost flat. Once loading is complete, the pilot starts the engines, and the fans rotate and suck in air. This is forced down into the skirt under the craft so the hovercraft is floating on a cushion of air. Power is then sent to the propellers, which make the hovercraft move forward. Hovercraft cruise at about 80km per hour, with only the edge of the skirt touching the surface.

The first hovercraft was invented by Sir Christopher Cockerell in 1959. It flew from the Isle of Wight to mainland England. Hovercraft are of most use in countries where travel is difficult and there are few roads. They can be used to go up rivers, over ice and across deserts.

Heinemann Literacy World

(Exemplar analysis)

Example of analysis of an explanation text

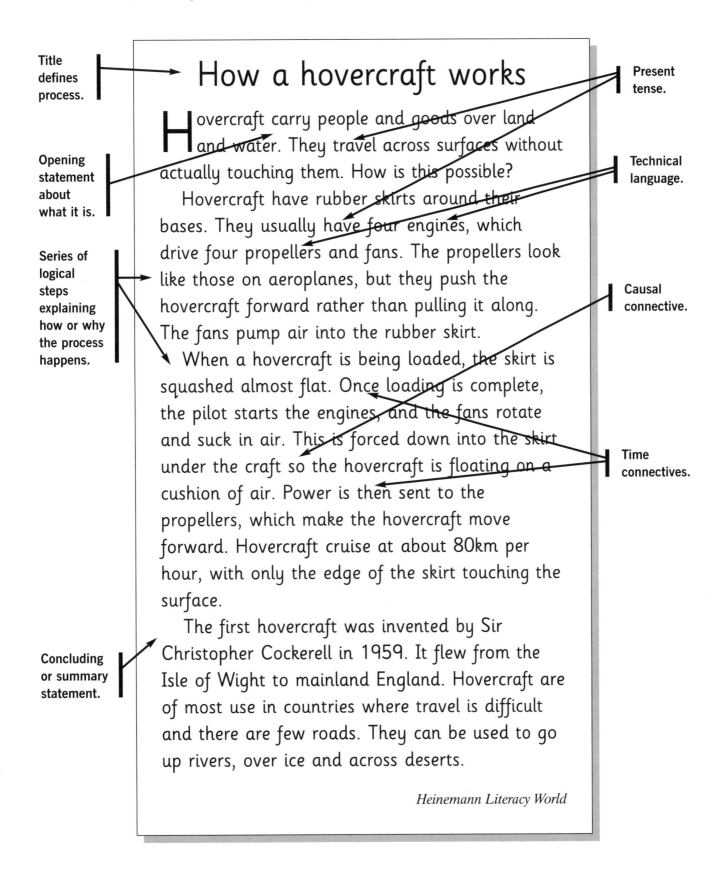

Title defines process.

Opening statement about what it is.

Series of logical steps explaining how or why the process happens.

Concluding or summary statement.

How a hovercraft works

Hovercraft carry people and goods over land and water. They travel across surfaces without actually touching them. How is this possible?

Hovercraft have rubber skirts around their bases. They usually have four engines, which drive four propellers and fans. The propellers look like those on aeroplanes, but they push the hovercraft forward rather than pulling it along. The fans pump air into the rubber skirt.

When a hovercraft is being loaded, the skirt is squashed almost flat. Once loading is complete, the pilot starts the engines, and the fans rotate and suck in air. This is forced down into the skirt under the craft so the hovercraft is floating on a cushion of air. Power is then sent to the propellers, which make the hovercraft move forward. Hovercraft cruise at about 80km per hour, with only the edge of the skirt touching the surface.

The first hovercraft was invented by Sir Christopher Cockerell in 1959. It flew from the Isle of Wight to mainland England. Hovercraft are of most use in countries where travel is difficult and there are few roads. They can be used to go up rivers, over ice and across deserts.

Heinemann Literacy World

Present tense.

Technical language.

Causal connective.

Time connectives.

Classworks Literacy Year 4 © Sue Plechowicz, Nelson Thornes Ltd 2003

(**Pupil copymaster**)

A text for you to analyse

Where do rivers come from?

A river is a length of fresh water flowing in a channel towards the sea. Rivers of all sizes flow in all areas of the world. But where do rivers come from?

The length or course of a river can be divided into three sections - the upper, middle and lower courses. The upper course is where the river starts. This is known as the river's source. The source is always on high ground, usually in the hills or mountains, but some rivers, like the Nile in Africa, have a lake as their source.

The most usual source for a river is a spring bubbling up from the underground. These underground springs are caused by rain seeping down through the soil and rocks until it meets a layer of rocks that cannot hold any more water. As a result the water begins to flow back out of the ground.

Other river sources are the result of melting snow and ice. When the weather gets warmer it causes the ice and snow to melt and trickle over the surface of the land. Then the trickles join up to form tiny streams that flow downhill.

As they continue their downhill journey, the streams that flow from surface water and from springs gradually meet together and grow into a large, fast-flowing river.

Classworks Literacy Year 4 © Sue Plechowicz, Nelson Thornes Ltd 2003

(Exemplar material)

Modelled explanation

How does an oxbow lake form?

Lakes are large areas of water surrounded by land. Some unusual lakes are found alongside the middle and lower courses of rivers. These are horseshoe or crescent-shaped and are known as oxbow lakes. Although most lakes are formed by water gathering in large hollows in the ground, the formation of oxbow lakes is different.

How are these strange lakes formed?

Once a river leaves the mountains and hills it reaches flatter land and as a result it flows more slowly. However it is still powerful. When there is an obstacle in its way it flows around it, cutting sideways into the riverbank. This causes the river to twist in huge bends called meanders. On the inner side of the meander the river drops some of the mud and sand that it has been carrying but the pressure of the water continues to erode the outer side of the meander. The result is that the loop becomes very big and the neck may become very narrow.

When the river floods the water may take a short cut across the narrow neck of the meander, softening the remaining land. Eventually it becomes eroded so that the river course is changed. Silt then builds up and permanently cuts off the horseshoe section of the meander. This is an oxbow lake.

An abandoned meander or oxbow lake is surrounded by fertile mud and silt, making it a very good place for plants and wildlife. If you are a nature lover, look out for an oxbow lake – it will be sure to offer you a good deal of enjoyment.

(**Pupil copymaster**)

Sentence cards

an abandoned meander
or oxbow lake
surrounded
fertile mud and silt
very good for plants and wildlife
making it
being

is	by
,	,

(Exemplar material)

Checklist and models for explanations and information books

Example of a checklist for writing explanations ①

Structure

- Title indicates what you are writing about; 'How ...' or 'Why ...' helps

- Opening statement introduces the topic and addresses reader

- A series of logical steps explains how or why something happens

- Often includes diagrams or photographs

- Concluding summary or statement relates subject to reader

- Additional information may be provided in boxes

- May need a glossary

Language features

- Use present tense

- Use time connectives

- Use causal connectives

- Use technical language

Example of a modelled information box ②

An abandoned meander or oxbow lake is also sometimes known as a bayou.

Example of a modelled glossary ③

Erode – Wear away land

Fertile – Land that is fertile has soil that is full of nutrients which plants need to grow well

Meanders – Bends in a river

Riverbank – The sides of a river

Silt – Tiny pieces of mud and rock that settle at the bottom of rivers

Classworks Literacy Year 4 © Sue Plechowicz, Nelson Thornes Ltd 2003

(Pupil copymaster)

Name: _____

Pupil	Objective	Teacher
	My title 'How ...' or 'Why ...' indicates what I am writing about.	
	My opening statement introduces the topic and addresses the reader.	
	A series of logical steps explains how or why something happens.	
	I have included a diagram.	
	My concluding summary or statement relates the subject to the reader.	
	I have given additional information in boxes.	
	I have used the present tense.	
	I have used time and causal connectives.	
	My glossary explains technical language.	
	What could I do to improve my work next time?	

Discussion Texts

Outcome

Points of view, sequenced in a writing frame, ready for a presentation or debate; a discussion text

Objectives

Sentence

4 the use of connectives, e.g. adverbs, adverbial phrases, conjunctions, to structure an argument.

Text

16 to read, compare and evaluate examples of arguments and discussions, e.g. letters to press, articles, discussion of issues in books, e.g. environment, animal welfare.

17 [be taught] how arguments are presented, e.g. ordering points to link them together so that one follows from another.

21 to assemble and sequence points in order to plan the presentation of a point of view.

22 to use writing frames if necessary to back up points of view with illustrations and examples.

24 to summarise in writing the key ideas from, e.g. a paragraph or chapter.

Planning frame

- Read and analyse discussion text.
- Express opinions on an issue.
- Plan for and against arguments on frame.
- Write a discussion about an issue.
- Link arguments using connectives.
- Prepare and present a discussion as a court case.

How you could plan this unit

Day 1	Day 2	Day 3	Day 4	Day 5
Reading and analysis	**Writing**	**Reading and analysis** Identify language features in Resource Page A (see Resource Page B). Start checklist (see Resource Page E). The children annotate Resource Page C. Plenary: add to checklist	**Speaking and listening** Identify topical issues to discuss. The children express opinions. Plan pros and cons about school uniform and discuss. Report in plenary	**Writing**
Structural Features	*Planning Grids*			*More Planning Grids*

Day 6	Day 7	Day 8	Day 9	Day 10
Writing Model how to write introduction and final statement (Resource Page D). The children write own introductions and final statements. Plenary: share work	**Writing** List arguments for and against selling fruit or sweets to raise money for new computer. Discuss linking arguments using connectives. The children find effective ways to start each sentence	**Writing** *Writing a Text*	**Evaluating** Model how to evaluate using a marking ladder (Resource Page F). The children mark own text and make final copy for writing folder. Plenary: share work	**Speaking and listening** Review discussion texts, focusing on language use. In groups, the children prepare a talk, including introduction, arguments for and against and final statement. Plenary: groups give talks

Day 11	Day 12	Day 13	Day 14	Day 15
Speaking and listening	**Speaking and listening** Presenting court case	**Speaking and listening** Presenting court case	**Speaking and listening** Presenting court case	**Speaking and listening** Presenting court case
A Court Case				

Structural Features

Objective

We will read and analyse examples of arguments and discussions

You need: Resource Pages A–C and E; highlighters.

Whole class work

- Introduce genre and purpose: ***A discussion text presents arguments and information from different viewpoints.***

- In pairs, give the children a couple of minutes to consider how a discussion text is different from a persuasive text.

- Establish that discussion texts offer both sides of an argument, whereas persuasive texts only state one side or someone's opinion.

- Read Resource Page A, asking the children to concentrate on the text structure.

- Together, annotate the text (see Resource Page B).

- Establish that the text opens with a clear statement about the issue under discussion. Add to a class checklist of structural features (see Resource Page E for ideas).

- Identify that the main body of a discussion text offers arguments for and against the issue that are frequently supported with evidence. Note that the text ends with a concluding statement. Add these two points to your class checklist.

Independent, pair or guided work

- In pairs, the children identify the structure of another discussion text (Resource Page C), and annotate using highlighters.

Plenary

- Share work, ensuring that the children have identified structural features from the class checklist.

Planning Grids

Objective

We will identify arguments for and against an issue and record on a planning grid

You need: Resource Pages A and C; individual whiteboards.

Whole class work	• Introduce the learning objectives for this lesson.

• Review the difference between 'persuasive' and 'discussion' text.

• Using the example below as a basis, discuss with the children what the planning frame for a discussion text might look like. Sketch one on the board, explaining your actions. Establish that the best frame is a 'for' and 'against' grid.

FOR	AGAINST

Collaborate on placing the following arguments for and against zoos from Resource Page A on to the grid:

> Watching animals on TV is different from real life.
>
> They are educational.
>
> Endangered species can be saved by breeding programmes.
>
> Scientists can study and research.
>
> Can watch animals in natural habitats on TV.
>
> Cruel to capture and transport animals.
>
> Cruel to keep them in cages.

Independent, pair or guided work

• In pairs, the children highlight for and against arguments from Resource Page C in different colours and place on their own planning grid.

Plenary

• Review the children's work, ensuring arguments are correctly placed on the grid.

More Planning Grids

Objective

We will present arguments for and against an issue using a planning grid

You need: individual whiteboards; large sheet of paper; selection of class discussion texts.

Whole class work

- Introduce the idea that the children are going to discuss arguments for and against having swimming lessons in school time.

- Ask the children to discuss 'for' arguments with their response partner. (Allow one minute.)

- Display some of these ideas on a large planning grid.

- Ask the children to write one argument against swimming lessons on their whiteboard. Discuss some of their reasons and record on the class planning grid:

FOR	AGAINST
Safety around rivers, sea and lakes. Good exercise. Fun.	Too much time taken travelling. Parents have to pay. Some children self-conscious about changing.

Independent, pair or guided work

- Brainstorm some topical issues of interest to the children that they can research or that they have enough knowledge of that they will be able to write both sides of an argument. For example:

  > At what age should children have mobile phones?
  >
  > Should children walk to school rather than come by car?

- Alternatively, provide a selection of discussion texts from your library.

- The children choose an issue and place arguments for and against on a planning grid.

Plenary

- Share some work, asking the children to evaluate using a response sandwich: one good comment; one area for improvement; another good comment.

Writing a Text

Objective

We will write the main part of our discussion text

You need: Resource Page D.

Whole class work	● Introduce how to use connectives (*Grammar for Writing*, Unit 32).
	● Model how to use a for and against grid to support the writing of the main body of your discussion text (Resource Page D). Ensure you refer to your class checklist constantly, explaining the decisions you make and orally rehearsing your choices.
	● Focus on the use of connectives to link your arguments. The children use whiteboards to brainstorm a list of connectives.
Independent, pair or guided work	● The children write the main body of their own discussion text, using the points from their for and against grids, and providing evidence (where possible) for their arguments.
Plenary	● Share some work, asking the children to evaluate by referring to the checklist.

A Court Case

Objective

We will prepare arguments for and against an issue for a mock court case

You need: Resource Page E.

Whole class work

- Brainstorm some issues. These can be the ones children worked on individually, but you may prefer to cover topical local or national issues.

- Decide on an issue to present to an audience in the form of a court case.

- Explain that you are going to act out a court case, putting your issue on trial.

- Allocate parts as follows:
  - a court official to introduce the case – similar to the introduction in a written discussion text
  - at least three defence witnesses – using 'for' arguments, each with their own lawyer to introduce them
  - at least three prosecution witnesses – as above, using 'against' arguments
  - a judge to sum up (summarise arguments) – similar to the concluding statement in a written discussion text.

- The remainder of the class will play additional lawyers, able to ask one question each. This is a Speaking and Listening objective and will also allow witnesses to give supporting evidence.

Independent, pair or guided work

- Prepare the court case as a whole class, starting by compiling a for and against grid.

- Ensure that language features from the checklist (Resource Page E) are used orally.

- Present the court case as an assembly to the rest of the school, who could then act as the jury, voting on the issue.

A discussion text

Do we still need zoos?

Zoos were originally set up so that people could see and learn about the wild animals from distant lands. As more people became city-dwellers, never seeing animals in the wild, zoos began to house local creatures too.

However, in today's world, are zoos really necessary?

Since people can now see any sort of wild animal in its natural habitat, simply by tuning in to a TV programme or buying a video, some animal rights' activists claim that zoos are out of date. They argue that it is cruel to capture animals, transport them long distances, and then keep them caged up, simply for the entertainment of human beings. Captive animals often develop 'zoochosis' – abnormal behaviour like rocking or swaying – which indicates that they are bored and unhappy in their prison-like conditions.

On the other hand, there is a huge difference between watching an animal on screen and seeing it in real life. It could be argued that visiting a zoo is educational, often increasing people's concern for wildlife and conservation, which is of great importance in today's developing – and often overdeveloped – world. Indeed, sometimes the only way to save an endangered species may be to arrange for it to breed in captivity. Behind the scenes, zoos also provide scientists with opportunities to research into animal behaviour: modern zoos can therefore be much better planned than old-fashioned ones, providing animals with carefully designed enclosures appropriate to their needs.

It seems, then, that there are still arguments for retaining zoos. These should, however, be carefully planned with the animals' welfare in mind: in the modern world, there is no excuse for keeping animals in cramped or cruel conditions.

Sue Palmer

(Exemplar analysis)

Example of analysis of a discussion text

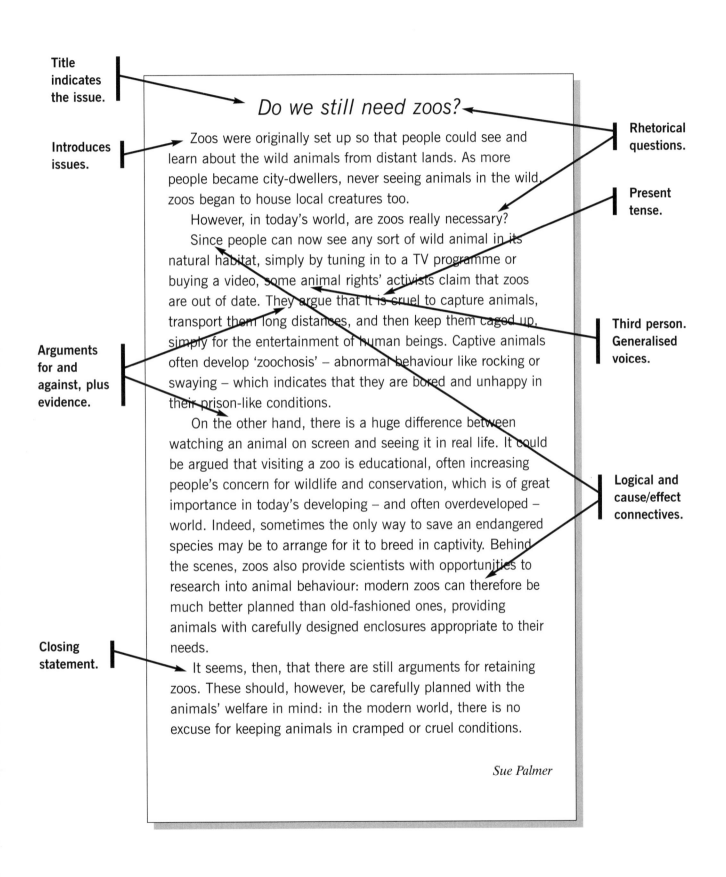

Title indicates the issue.

Introduces issues.

Arguments for and against, plus evidence.

Closing statement.

Do we still need zoos?

Zoos were originally set up so that people could see and learn about the wild animals from distant lands. As more people became city-dwellers, never seeing animals in the wild, zoos began to house local creatures too.

However, in today's world, are zoos really necessary? Since people can now see any sort of wild animal in its natural habitat, simply by tuning in to a TV programme or buying a video, some animal rights' activists claim that zoos are out of date. They argue that it is cruel to capture animals, transport them long distances, and then keep them caged up, simply for the entertainment of human beings. Captive animals often develop 'zoochosis' – abnormal behaviour like rocking or swaying – which indicates that they are bored and unhappy in their prison-like conditions.

On the other hand, there is a huge difference between watching an animal on screen and seeing it in real life. It could be argued that visiting a zoo is educational, often increasing people's concern for wildlife and conservation, which is of great importance in today's developing – and often overdeveloped – world. Indeed, sometimes the only way to save an endangered species may be to arrange for it to breed in captivity. Behind the scenes, zoos also provide scientists with opportunities to research into animal behaviour: modern zoos can therefore be much better planned than old-fashioned ones, providing animals with carefully designed enclosures appropriate to their needs.

It seems, then, that there are still arguments for retaining zoos. These should, however, be carefully planned with the animals' welfare in mind: in the modern world, there is no excuse for keeping animals in cramped or cruel conditions.

Sue Palmer

Rhetorical questions.

Present tense.

Third person. Generalised voices.

Logical and cause/effect connectives.

Classworks Literacy Year 4 © Sue Plechowicz, Nelson Thornes Ltd 2003

195

A discussion text for you to analyse

Should children wear school uniform?

Many thousands of children in the UK attend schools where they have to wear a school uniform. However, it is often a hotly debated issue with both parents and pupils asking, should school uniforms be compulsory?

Those people who think that school uniforms are a good thing, suggest that they give pupils a feeling of belonging but others argue that everyone should be treated as individuals who are free to choose what they want to wear so that they can express themselves.

Teachers often say that having a uniform is good since it makes pupils immediately recognisable which is much safer when on school trips or outings.

Sometimes children don't like their uniform. Indeed some may feel very uncomfortable in the particular style chosen by the school. This may mean that they are unable to concentrate and work properly. However parents frequently say that they are relieved that their children have to wear a uniform so that they don't have to deal with arguments about buying the latest fashions for children to show off at school.

On the other hand, some parents complain that it is hard to keep their children looking clean and smart because they often get their school uniform dirty and it is very difficult to wash and dry it by the next day.

It seems then that there are sensible reasons on both sides of the argument as to whether school uniforms should be compulsory and it is probably an issue that will continue to be hotly debated by individuals.

Classworks Literacy Year 4 © Sue Plechowicz, Nelson Thornes Ltd 2003

(**Pupil copymaster**)

Modelled discussion text

Should swimming be part of the school timetable?

The National Curriculum for Physical Education states that swimming activities and water safety must be taught in primary schools. However, is it really necessary for all children to learn to swim at school?

Very few primary schools have swimming pools of their own and so in order to teach swimming, teachers have to take their pupils to the local leisure centre. This can take up a lot of time. Researchers have found that children are often away from the school for several hours but they spend less than half this time learning to swim. Some teachers and parents argue that too much teaching time is wasted on swimming days and suggest that swimming should be taught in after-school clubs or by parents.

Furthermore, many schools have to ask parents to contribute towards the cost of swimming lessons. This is because the hire of the pool and transport is very expensive. Some parents say they would prefer to spend the money taking their children themselves so that all the family can enjoy swimming together.

Some people suggest that being able to swim is only important if you live near the sea or a river and so only these children need to have swimming lessons at school. However, since most people come into contact with the sea, rivers, lakes or a pool at some time in their lives everyone does learn to be safe. If they don't learn at school the worry is that they may not be taught at all.

A lot of children enjoy swimming, it is a good way to exercise and can be a great deal of fun. However, others do not, because they feel very self-conscious about their bodies and do not want to wear costumes in front of their classmates. Is it fair to insist that they do so?

It seems that there are good arguments for ensuring that all children are taught to swim but whether this should be done in school hours is something that continues to be debated.

Checklist for discussion texts

Structure

- Open with a clear statement of the issue

- Give arguments for and against with supporting evidence

- Give a concluding statement

Language features

- Use present tense

- Use third person and generalised voices

- Use logical and cause and effect connectives

Marking ladder

Name: _____

Pupil	Objective	Teacher
	I used a clear opening statement.	
	I gave arguments for and against.	
	I supported the arguments with evidence.	
	I used a concluding statement.	
	I used the present tense and third person.	
	I linked arguments and paragraphs using connectives.	
	What could I do to improve my work next time?	

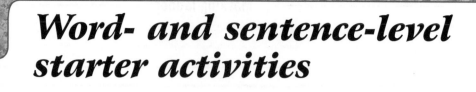

Word- and sentence-level starter activities

Simple games

- Play games in teams of four, each team with a collection of about 60 cards, for example, 20 with word roots and 40 with derivations from them. Some games to play:
  - Sort the cards into correct groups. Which team was quickest?
  - Sort according to spelling patterns/word types (nouns, adjectives, and so on) **Can you make a comment?** (For example, 'None of the words associated with "child" is a verb.')
  - Ask the children to devise their own group games. For example, Two for a Goal: each child in a group of four has two word roots, which are kept in individual 'banks'. The remaining cards are placed in a central pile, and the children take turns turning the top one over, either keeping it or returning it to the bottom of the pile. (No one may ever hold more than two cards at once.) When you have a root and two associated words, this scores a run and you call 'GOAL!' Keep the run in your bank and work on your second root word. The game is over when someone scores two goals, or when everyone is 'stuck'. (In this case, hold a 'sudden death play-off', in which all cards are reshuffled, placed in one pile, turned over one at a time, and the first person to hold a root word and one of its associated words wins. Only two words can be held by a player, so they must constantly decide whether to keep or put back.)

I'm a Dalek

- Speak robotically, dividing speech into syllables. For example, 'I be/lieve in a/li/ens. Do you be/lieve? Are you an ... a/li/en? Do you ... be/lieve?' (Point to a child and ask them to write up the word correctly. Celebrate correct spellings. Continue with two- and three-syllable words related to literacy texts or other curriculum areas, for example, 'mon/ster'; 'hap/py'; 'pers/on'; 'treas/ure'; 'com/put/er'.

I Spy

- Play 'I Spy' focusing on a recently met sound or letter string. The clue must have the first letter and one other numbered letter, for example, 'I spy ... something beginning with "p", and the third letter is "o".' Make constant rule changes to the clue, for example, stating the first letter and last two, the initial letter and the last letter, the initial letter and the number of syllables, and so on.

Building blocks

- Who is in on the act? Give pairs of children the two-minute challenge of writing as many words as they can containing 'act', for example, 'react'; 'actor'; 'activate'; 'activity'; 'action'; 'reaction'. Repeat the process with other simple words that appear in other words, for example: 'do'; 'take'; 'hand'; 'hero'; 'call'. **Are any spelling rules coming into play?** (for example, 'take' in 'overtaking'). Encourage the use of dictionaries.

How am I doing?

- Ask the children to focus on spellings they need more practice with, for example, words they often get wrong in literacy writing; words from their spelling logs. They should write a list of words (about 15) to learn during the week. Brainstorm strategies for learning, for example, applying known spelling conventions/rules; considering the look of a word; pronunciation ('later' or 'latter'); trying and testing; devising mnemonics; and so on.

Strange People Eat Lettuce Leaves In Night Gear

- Brainstorm and display some silly mnemonics for class use. Use a class and homework session to devise some for a personal list.